OPEN
BOOK

Grammar

D1277527

Pearson Education ESL
Canadian Titles and Authors

Canadian Stories by Eleanor Adamowski

The Longman Picture Dictionary, Canadian ed., Julie Ashworth & John Clark

Reading for the Write Reasons: English Reading and Writing for Advanced ESL Students by Donna Aziz-Canuel, Lynne Gaetz & Richard Pawsey

Amazing! News Interviews & Conversations by Susan Bates

Amazing Canadian Newspaper Stories by Susan Bates

Amazing 2! News Interviews & Conversations by Susan Bates

Amazing 2! Canadian Newspaper Stories by Susan Bates

Canadian Concepts, 2nd ed., Books 1-6 by Lynda Berish & Sandra Thibaudeau

English Fast Forward 1, 2nd ed., by Lynda Berish & Sandra Thibaudeau

English Fast Forward 2, 2nd ed., by Lynda Berish & Sandra Thibaudeau

English Fast Forward 3, 2nd ed., by Lynda Berish & Sandra Thibaudeau

Grammar Connections, Books 1, 2 & 3, by Lynda Berish & Sandra Thibaudeau

On Target by Keith L. Boeckner & Joan Polfuss Boeckner

On Target Too by Keith L. Boeckner & Joan Polfuss Boeckner

Target Practice by Keith L. Boeckner & Joan Polfuss Boeckner

Classics Canada: Authentic Readings for ESL Students, Books 1-4, by Patricia Brock & Brian John Busby

Coming to Canada: Authentic Reading for ESL Students by Patricia Brock & Brian John Busby

Contemporary Canada: Authentic Readings for ESL Students by Patricia Brock & Brian John Busby

Being Canadian: Language for Citizenship by Judy Cameron & Tracey M. Derwing

Focus 2: Academic Listening and Speaking Skills by Ranka Curcin, Mary Koumoulas, & Sonia Fiorucci-Nicholls

Focus 2: Academic Reading Skills by Ranka Curcin, Mary Koumoulas, & Sonia Fiorucci-Nicholls

Focus 2: Academic Writing Skills by Ranka Curcin, Mary Koumoulas, & Sonia Fiorucci-Nicholls

Writing for Success: Preparing for Business, Technology, Trades and Career Programs by Dale Fitzpatrick & Kathleen Center Vance

All Right!: A Guide to Correct English by Paul Fournier

English on Demand, 2nd ed., by Paul Fournier

English on Line, 2nd ed., by Paul Fournier

English on Purpose, 2nd ed., by Paul Fournier

This Side Up by Paul Fournier

This Way Out by Paul Fournier

Before Brass Tacks: Basic Grammar by Lynne Gaetz

Before Brass Tacks: Basic Skills in English by Lynne Gaetz

Brass Ring 1: Basic English for Career-Related Communication by Lynne Gaetz

Brass Ring 1: Basic Grammar Review by Lynne Gaetz

Brass Ring 2: English for Career-Related Communication by Lynne Gaetz

Brass Ring 2: Grammar Review by Lynne Gaetz

Brass Tacks Grammar by Lynne Gaetz

Brass Tacks: Integrated Skills in English by Lynne Gaetz

Open Book English Skills by Lynne Gaetz

Open Book Grammar by Lynne Gaetz

Open Road English Skills by Lynne Gaetz

Open Road Grammar by Lynne Gaetz

Open Window English Skills by Lynne Gaetz

Open Window Grammar by Lynne Gaetz

Bridge to Fluency by Elizabeth Gatbonton

Links: ESL Writing and Editing by Carolyn Greene & Claudia Rock

A Beginning Look at Canada by Anne-Marie Kaskens

A Canadian Conversation Book: English in Everyday Life, 2nd ed., Book 1, by Tina Kasloff Carver, Sandra Douglas Fotinos & Clarice Cooper

Reading Matters: A Selection of Canadian Writing by Jane Merivale

Word-by-Word Beginning Workbook, Canadian ed., by Steven Molinsky & Bill Bliss

Word-by-Word Intermediate Workbook, Canadian ed. by Steven Molinsky & Bill Bliss

Word-by-Word Picture Dictionary, Canadian ed. by Steven Molinsky & Bill Bliss

Take Charge: Using Everyday Canadian English by Lucia Pietrusiak Engkent

Take Part: Speaking Canadian English, 2nd ed., by Lucia Pietrusiak Engkent & Karen P. Bardy

Technically Speaking…: Writing, Reading and Listening, English at Work by Susan Quirk Drolet & Ann Farrell Séguin

Style and Substance: A Multimedia Approach to Literature and Composition by Claudia Rock & Suneeti Phadke

Read on Canada by Paul Sharples & Judith Clark

Getting it Together, Books 1 & 2, by Véra Téophil Naber

A Grammar Manual, Volumes A & B, by Véra Téophil Naber & Savitsa Sévigny

Advanced Half-Hour Helper: Puzzles and Activities for ESL Students by Joan Roberta White

Half-Hour Helper: Puzzles and Activities for ESL Students by Joan Roberta White

Making the Grade: An Interactive Course in English for Academic Purposes by David Wood

OPEN
BOOK

LYNNE GAETZ

LOW-INTERMEDIATE LEVEL

Grammar

Pearson
Education ESL

E RPI

DISTRIBUTED BY ÉDITIONS DU RENOUVEAU PÉDAGOGIQUE INC.

5757, RUE CYPIHOT
SAINT-LAURENT (QUÉBEC)
H4S 1R3

TÉLÉPHONE : (514) 334-2690
TÉLÉCOPIEUR : (514) 334-4720
COURRIEL : erpidlm@erpi.com

Project Editor:
Joyce Rappaport

Illustrations:
Stéphane Jorisch

Book design and page layout:
diabolo-menthe

Registration of copyright: 2nd quarter 2002
Bibliothèque nationale du Québec
National Library of Canada
Imprimé au Canada

ISBN 2-7613-1340-2
1234567890 II 098765432
30080 ABCD   OF2-10

Acknowledgements

I would like to express sincere thanks to:

- Claudia Rock and Joyce Rappaport for their invaluable
  editing.
- Jean-Pierre Albert, Julie Champoux, and the team
  at diabolo-menthe.
- All of my colleagues at Collège Lionel-Groulx. They are
  truly a comfortable and inspiring group of people to
  work with.
- Everyone who agreed to be interviewed for the book.
- My colleagues throughout the province who kindly
  provided feedback:
  Ann Kelly, Cégep Abitimi-Témiscamingue
  Geraldine Arbach, Collège de l'outaouais
  Peggy Swan Bérubé, Institut Maritime du Québec
  Barbara Fraser, Collège Ahuntsic
  Hugh Bourgoyne, Cégep de St-Jérôme
  Deborah Albert, UVCS, English Language Centre,
  Continuing Studies, BC

Finally, I would like to extend special thanks to my
husband and children.

Table of Contents

OPEN BOOK Grammar

UNIT 1 General Review

UNIT 2 Pronouns

UNIT 3 Simple Present

UNIT 4 Present Progressive

UNIT 5 Simple Past

UNIT 6 Past Progressive

Review of Units 1 to 6

UNIT 7 Plurals and Articles

UNIT 8 Future Tenses

UNIT 9 Modals

UNIT 10 Comparisons

UNIT 11 Word Choice

UNIT 12 Spelling and Punctuation

Review of Units 7 to 12

Grammar Appendix

© Longman

1 General Review

(Parts of Speech, Sentences, Prepositions)

The Parts of Speech

EXERCISE 1 Look carefully at the following sets of words. The word groups contain examples of certain parts of speech. (In the Grammar Charts, there is a complete list of the parts of speech with definitions for each term.)

Label each set of words with one of the following terms.

nouns	verbs	adverbs	adjectives
pronouns	prepositions	articles	

EXAMPLE: men, book, Mr. Roy, candle   These are _____*nouns*_____

1. of, in, on, above, at, for, about, with, below   These are _____

2. the, a, an   These are _____

3. slowly, unfortunately, sadly, often, always, easily   These are _____

4. handsome, wonderful, old, thin, serious, loud, cute   These are _____

5. I, you, we, she, he, it, they, him, theirs   These are _____

6. walk, run, sweep, drive, mow, drink, endure, skip   These are _____

7. Mr. Finch, Elm Street, bottles, dictionary, Mexico   These are _____

SENTENCES

A complete sentence has a subject and a verb.

It   is   cold in February.
subject   verb

Avoid Double Subjects
When you state the subject of a sentence, it is not necessary to repeat the subject in the pronoun form.

Incorrect: My partner, ~~she~~ is very nice.
Correct: My partner is nice.

EXERCISE 2 Carefully correct the following sentences. Some sentences have no subject or verb, and some sentences have a double subject.

EXAMPLE:

                          are

Some people ↑ very funny.

1. Many famous comedians they are from Canada.

2. Jim Carrey and Mike Myers from Ontario.

3. Jim lived in Newmarket, Ontario, when was younger.

4. Comedy it is very difficult to do.

5. I like Mike Myers because is a funny comedian.

6. Canada it also produces many great musicians.

7. The woman with long black hair a very good musician.

8. Alanis she has a very good voice.

9. Alternative music is great because is very innovative.

10. Music and laughter very important.

Prepositions

■ IN, ON, AT, AND TO

The following diagram indicates when you can use *in*, *on*, *at*, and *to* most of the time.

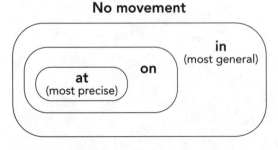

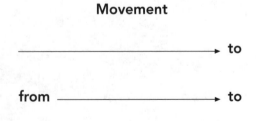

EXAMPLE: *I live **in** Calgary, **on** Maple Street.*

                                          *Everyday I drive **to** school.*

PREPOSITIONS OF TIME		PREPOSITIONS OF PLACE	
In	• in 1989 (in a year) • in July (in a month) Also: • in the morning / afternoon / evening • in the spring / fall / summer / winter	In	• in Boston (in a city) • in Spain (in a country)
On	• on Monday (on a day of the week) • on June 16 (on a specific date) Also: • on time (meaning "punctual") • on my birthday	On	• on 17th Avenue (on a street) Also: • on TV • on the radio • on the phone
At	• at 8:30 (at a specific time of day) • at night	At	• at 15 Laval Road (at a specific address) • at the hospital (at a specific building)
From ... to	• from 6 AM to 8 PM (from one period to another)	From ... to	• from Chile to Canada (from one place to another)

EXERCISE 3 Put *in*, *on*, or *at* in the spaces provided.

1. _____*in*_____ the morning

2. _____ the phone

3. _____ 32 Ocean Drive

4. _____ Spain

5. _____ Pine Avenue

6. _____ 1994

7. _____ September

8. _____ a month

9. _____ September 12

10. _____ midnight

11. _____ the television

12. _____ my birthday

EXERCISE 4 Fill in the blanks with the appropriate prepositions for time and place. You can use *in*, *on*, *at*, or *from ... to*.

1. Jim Carrey was born _____ the winter. To be more specific, he was born _____ January 17, _____ the year 1962. Jim worked at a comedy club _____ Toronto _____ 1977 _____ 1979. The club, called Yuk Yuks, is _____ 2335 Yonge Street.

2. _____ September, 1990, he appeared _____ television in a show called "In Living Color." Then, _____ 1994, Jim made the movie, *Ace Ventura, Pet Detective*.

3. Tonight I will watch *The Truman Show* _____ television. The movie starts _____ 9 PM.

4. When Jim Carrey was seven years old, humans first walked on the moon. _____ July 20, 1969, Neil Armstrong took that first step on the moon's surface. The event appeared _____ TV and the astronauts talked about it _____ the radio. _____ 9:30 _____ the morning, Jim watched the astronauts.

TO vs. AT

To: generally used after verbs that indicate movement from one place *to* another. Generally use *to* after the following verbs:

go to	walk to	run to	move to	return to

EXCEPTION   Do not put *to* before "home." *I'll go home with you.*

At: used after verbs that indicate stillness. Use *at* after the following verbs:

wait at	stay at	sit at	look at	work at

EXERCISE 5   Write *at, to,* or X *(meaning no preposition is needed)* in the spaces provided.

EXAMPLE: This week the boss is staying _____*at*_____ the Ritz Hotel in Vancouver.

1. The students want to go _____ New York in October.

2. Please wait _____ the entrance of the museum.

3. In the museum, I looked _____ the paintings of Vincent Van Gogh.

4. Last year we went _____ Mexico for two weeks.

5. Could you please go _____ home now. This bar is closed.

6. My sister goes with her friends _____ a coffee shop every Saturday.

7. He always jogs _____ that restaurant. He sits _____ a table near a window and he looks _____ the scenery outside. Then he walks _____ home.

8. Every summer, I work _____ a supermarket. I drive _____ work.

9. Next year we will move _____ Nebraska. We will stay _____ my brother's house until we find an apartment.

10. Last week Mr. Laurin went _____ the meeting in Ottawa.

Take Another Look

Answer the following questions. If you don't know an answer, then go back and review the appropriate section.

1. Put *in*, *on*, or *at* in the spaces provided.

   _____ 1995   _____ night   _____ Mexico   _____ the telephone

   _____ 5 PM   _____ March 15   _____ TV   _____ Vancouver

2. What preposition follows verbs such as *go, run,* and *walk*?

   a) to   **b)** at

3. What preposition follows verbs such as *sit, wait,* and *stay*?

   a) to   **b)** at

CLASS EXERCISE (REVIEW)

PART A: Circle the letter of the best answer.

1. The politicians went . . . Quebec City to discuss global trade.

   a) to   **b)** at   **c)** (nothing)

2. The meeting was . . . April 20, 2001.

   a) in   **b)** on   **c)** at

3. The government officials met . . . 9 PM.

   a) in   **b)** on   **c)** at

4. Each year protesters go . . . the trade conference.

   a) at   **b)** to   **c)** in

5. At the 2001 conference, people protested . . . St. Jean Street.

   a) in   **b)** on   **c)** at

6. Next year the conference will be . . . Mexico.

   a) in   **b)** on   **c)** at

7. The delegates will stay . . . a very expensive hotel.

   a) to   **b)** on   **c)** at

PART B: Correct the sentence error. (There may be a missing word or a double subject.)

EXAMPLE:

it

I like the west coast because ↑ is very beautiful.

8. The best thing about Italy the great art.

9. Emily Carr she painted totem poles.

10. I like that painting because is original.

2 Pronouns

	SUBJECT PRONOUNS	OBJECT PRONOUNS	POSSESSIVE ADJECTIVES*	POSSESSIVE PRONOUNS	REFLEXIVE PRONOUNS
	Subject pronouns replace the subject and are generally followed by a verb.

She is sleeping. | Object pronouns replace the object and are usually found after a verb or preposition.
*Mary saw **him** yesterday.* | Possessive adjectives describe a noun and appear before the noun that they describe.
*That is **our** car.* | Possessive pronouns indicate possession and *replace* a noun.

*That car is **ours**.* | Reflexive pronouns "reflect" back on the subject.

*You could do it by **yourself**.* |
| **Singular** | I
you
he
she
it | me
you
him
her
it | my
your
his
her
its | mine
yours
his
hers
— | myself
yourself
himself
herself
itself |
| **Plural** | we
you
they | us
you
them | our
your
their | ours
yours
theirs | ourselves
yourselves
themselves |

* Possessive Adjective Reminder

- When something belongs to an object, use *its*: *The car lost **its** wheel in the accident.*
- When something belongs to a woman, use *her*. *Anna took **her** car to the garage.*
- When something belongs to a man, use *his*. *Martin invited **his** mother to dinner.*

Subject and Object Pronouns

Sentences have a subject (the actor) and object (the thing affected by the action).

EXAMPLE: **She** didn't give **him** any advice.

      subject   object

EXERCISE 1 Replace the words in parentheses with a subject or object pronoun.

EXAMPLE: (Jane) _____*She*_____ will return the (video cassette) _____*it*_____.

1. Please give (that lottery ticket) _____ to (Audrey) _____.

2. There is mail for (you and me) _____.

3. (That nice lady) _____ inherited a lot of money from (her parents) _____ .

4. (Helen and Alfred) _____ work for (their father) _____ .

5. Helen does not like (her big house) _____ .

6. (My neighbor, Mrs. Rey) _____ works for (Alfred) _____ .

7. Mrs. Rey often invites (you and I) _____ for a visit.

8. (You and I) _____ must visit (your parents) _____ more often.

9. Audrey should ask (her employers) _____ to pay for (her new computer) _____ .

10. (Audrey) _____ uses (her computer) _____ everyday.

Possessive Adjectives

Possessive adjectives indicate possession and appear before the noun that they describe.
To choose the correct adjective, think about the possessor (not the object that is possessed).
For example, these are things that your sister "possesses": *her bedroom, her car, her keys,
her boyfriend, etc.*

The possessive adjectives are:

my	*your*	*his*	*her*	*its*	*our*	*their*

HIS vs. HER?

- When something belongs to a female, always use *her* (+ noun).
- When something belongs to a male, always use *his* (+ noun).

EXERCISE 2 Draw a line from the possessive adjective to the antecedent. The possessive adjectives are
in italics.

EXAMPLE: Mr. Chin gave **his** children some money. (The pronoun **his** relates to Mr. Chin.)

1. Club Morocco is famous for **its** rum drinks.

2. Rudy and Jane think that **their** club is very safe.

3. You sometimes bring *your* friends to that club.

4. We have problems with *our* neighbours. Club Morocco is beside *our* house. Some customers leave *their* motorcycles on *our* lawn.

5. I asked *my* friend about it. She told the story to *her* brother, the police officer. When he finishes *his* shift, he will speak to the club owners about the problem.

EXERCISE 3   Fill in the blanks with the correct possessive adjective.

EXAMPLE: Julie loves _____*her*_____ cats.

1. Mark wanted to do a nice thing for _____ grandmother. Last week Mark brought _____ grandmother on a trip to Alaska. He paid for _____ tickets with _____ credit card.

2. Mrs. Long invited _____ brother for Christmas dinner. He brought _____ wife and children to the dinner. After dinner, Mrs. Long gave _____ nieces and nephews some gifts.

3. Today many students like to travel. They fill _____ backpacks with clothing, and then they travel to distant countries.

4. Sandra went to Morocco with _____ best friend. Sandra didn't pay for the trip. She borrowed some money from _____ older brother Mark. Mark didn't want to give money to _____ sister. Eventually he agreed to give _____ sister the money.

5. My husband and I have two kids. We want to take _____ children to Miami next winter for a vacation.

THEIR / THERE / THEY'RE

The following words sound alike but have different meanings.

their:	possessive adjective	*The Smiths sold **their** house.*
they're:	they are (contraction)	*__They're__ very happy about it.*
there:	at that place; not here.	*Put the box over **there**.*
	also means "something exists"	*__There__ is a fly in my soup.*

EXERCISE 4 Put *their, they're,* or *there* in the spaces.

1. _____*There*_____ are three brothers who live in the apartment above me.

   I always ask them to turn _____ music down. I need to study for

   my tests.

2. _____ angry with me, but it is _____ fault. If

   _____ going to play loud music, then they have to deal with the

   consequences.

3. _____ are laws about noise levels. If they live in an apartment

   building where _____ are many neighbours, then they should

   understand that _____ are rules and regulations.

4. Yesterday they called _____ lawyer. I don't know what

   _____ lawyer told them, but last night _____ was

   no music coming from _____ apartment.

Possessive Pronouns

Possessive pronouns indicate ownership. They can replace the possessive adjective and noun.

<u>EXAMPLE:</u> *I lost my passport, but my parents found their passports.*
                                                    ‾‾‾‾‾‾‾‾‾‾
                                                      theirs

The possessive pronouns are:

   mine   *yours*   *his*   *hers*   *theirs*   *ours*

> ### THEIR vs. THEIRS?
> ### OUR vs. OURS?
>
> If the pronoun is followed by a noun, then use the form that does *not* end in *s*.
>
>   *their*
> <u>EXAMPLE:</u> *Andrew and Mark spent ~~theirs~~ money. We didn't spend ours.*

EXERCISE 5 In each sentence, circle the appropriate possessive adjective or pronoun.

<u>EXAMPLE:</u> I gave ((my), mine) old furniture to my younger sister.

1. We asked (our, ours) friends to visit (we, us, our, ours) during (their, theirs) vacation.

2. They asked if they could bring (their, theirs) skis along.

3. Alice invited (his, her) brother to join us.

4. Jeff Malone brought (his, her) own skis, but his wife left (her, hers) at home.

5. Alice brought (his, her) car, but we didn't bring (our, ours) because (it, he, she) was getting repaired.

6. At the ski lodge, everyone put (their, theirs) food on the table.

7. We shared everything. Some people ate (my, mine) food and I ate (their, theirs).

8. The Malones put (their, theirs) desserts on the table. I left (our, ours) in the kitchen.

9. Unfortunately, Alice broke (her, hers) leg during the ski vacation.

Possessive Case of Nouns ('s)

You can add *apostrophe –s ('s)* to nouns to indicate possession.

<u>EXAMPLE:</u>   *That is the child of Jerry. That is **Jerry's** child.*

If the noun is plural, then put the apostrophe after the *s*.

<u>EXAMPLE:</u>   *The **boys'** games are in the basement.*

If the noun has an irregular plural form, just add *'s* to the irregular form.

<u>EXAMPLE:</u>   *The **men's** room is down the hall.*

EXERCISE 6   Change the nouns to the possessive case.

<u>EXAMPLE:</u>   She is the sister of Josh.   She is _____ *Josh's sister* _____.

1. Those are the toys of the children.   Those are _____.

2. That is the snowboard of Mike.   That is _____.

3. That is the car of the Smiths.   That is _____.

4. He is the brother of Lisa.   He is _____.

5. That is the restroom of the women.   That is _____.

6. She is the mother of Ben.   She is _____.

EXERCISE 7   Write the possessive form of the noun in the spaces provided. The noun may require an apostrophe, or you may need to add *apostrophe –s*.

> **EXAMPLE:**   Diego*'s* _____ cat ran away.

1. **Simon**_____ mother visits the **Children**_____ Hospital every Monday.

2. **Ricky**_____ gift is always very expensive.

3. We have two dogs. The **dogs**_____ food bowls are in the kitchen.

4. Siri does the **company**_____ budget.

5. That firefighter saves many **people**_____ lives.

6. Her **mother**_____ sister lives in Florida.

7. What are those **men**_____ names?

8. The **girls**_____ clothes are in the closet.

Reflexive Pronouns

Reflexive pronouns are used when the subject doing the action and the object receiving the action are the same.

> *Jonathan is proud of **himself**.*

Reflexive pronouns reflect back on the subject. You cannot say *She likes himself*, because *himself* doesn't reflect back on the female subject *she*. Remember that *you* has both singular and plural reflexive pronouns.

     yourself   (one person: you)
     yourselves   (more than one person: you and others)

The expression *by + oneself* means "alone."

> **EXAMPLE:**   *I can do it by myself.*

EXERCISE 8   Write the correct reflexive pronoun in the space provided. Look at the chart at the beginning of this chapter if you need help with spelling.

> **EXAMPLE:**   I often talk to ___*myself*___ .

1. My boss, Mr. Griff, often talks to _____ .

2. We can finish the project by _____ .

3. The visitors should help _____ to coffee.

4. Do you want to do the job by _____ ?

5. I hope that you and your co-workers are proud of _____ .

■ THERE IS / THERE ARE

There is* means that something exists. *There is* a "false" subject, and the real subject follows the verb *be*.

There is *a tree in my yard.*   **There are** *many trees in the forest.*
There is (singular noun).   There are (plural noun).

Question form: Place *be* before "there."

Is there *a tree in my yard?*   **Are there** *many trees in the forest?*

* *There is* means "il y a" in French or "hay" in Spanish.

EXERCISE 9   Put "there is" or "there are" in the space provided. Then write the sentence in the form of a question.

EXAMPLE: _____*There are*_____ two mistakes in your text.

Are there two mistakes in your text?

1. _____ a police officer nearby.

   Question: _____

2. _____ many people on the subway.

   Question: _____

3. _____ a stop sign on the corner.

   Question: _____

4. _____ two donut shops on Main Street.

   Question: _____

THERE ARE, THEY ARE, AND *HE HAS*

Do not confuse "he has" or "they are" with *there are*. Note the differences between the following:

	MEANING	EXAMPLE
He has	A man possesses	*He has many friends.*
They are	Several people or things are	*They are in the coffee shop.*
There are	Something exists	*There are many people in the coffee shop.*

EXERCISE 10   Correct the errors in the following sentences. If the sentence is correct, write C in the space.

EXAMPLE: (He has) many clouds in the sky.   *There are*

1. They are many trains to Banff today. _____

2. There has a lot of interesting things to see there. _____

3. For example, there are many mountains surrounding the town. _____

4. There have a large lake nearby. _____

5. They are many wild animals in that region. _____

6. Don't feed the bears because they are wild animals. _____

7. Occasionally there have some bears in the town's streets. _____

8. They has many black bears in the Rocky Mountains. _____

CLASS EXERCISE

Describe your town or city. What attractions are there? Write five sentences using *there is* or *there are*.

FOR EXAMPLE: *There is a police station on Main Road.* _____

_____

_____

_____

_____

_____

Take Another Look

Answer the following questions. If you don't know an answer, then go back and review the appropriate section.

1. In the following sentence, do you put *our* or *ours* before the noun?

   That old Toyota is _____ car.

2. Circle two pronouns that are spelled *correctly*.

   theirselves   themselfs   themselves   thiers   theirs

3. Fill in the missing object pronouns. Complete the sentence: *Give it to…*

   a) I _____*me*_____   d) she _____

   b) you _____*you*_____   e) they _____

   c) he _____   f) we _____*us*_____

CLASS EXERCISE (REVIEW)

PART A: In each sentence, circle the correct term.

<u>EXAMPLE:</u>   I bought (*my*, *mine*) car at the Toyota dealer.

1. (*There are*, *They are*, *They have*) too many drivers with cellphones in this country.

2. We bought (*our*, *ours*) parents a cellphone to celebrate (*theirs*, *there*, *their*, *them*) anniversary.

3. They love the new cellphone. (*He*, *She*, *It*) works really well.

4. Today, I need to bring (*my*, *mine*, *me*) luggage to the airport.

5. Do you know where (*you*, *your*, *you're*) luggage is?

6. My sister asked (*his*, *her*, *hers*) travel agent to find a good deal.

7. Mr. Williams found cheap tickets to Nepal for (*we*, *our*, *us*).

8. We will spend (*our*, *ours*) vacation in Nepal.

9. (*There have*, *There are*, *They are*) many mountains in Nepal.

10. My sister will visit (*her*, *his*) boyfriend on his birthday. She will also give (*he*, *his*, *him*) a gift. Then she will catch (*her*, *hers*) flight to Nepal.

11. My parents should buy (*theirselves*, *themselves*, *themself*) tickets to Nepal.

12. My sister and I will go to Nepal by (*ourself*, *ourselves*).

PART B: Find the errors in the following paragraph. There are five errors with pronouns or possessive adjectives.

In most Canadian provinces, the eighteenth birthday is very special. Sarah's eighteenth birthday is tomorrow. She will celebrate her birthday with hers family and friends. First, Sarah will eat supper with her mother and father. Sarah's father will give hers a big birthday gift. Then Sarah will go to a club with hers friends. They will drink theirs beers until 3 AM. Sarah's boyfriend, Tony, will drive they home. Tony won't drink alcohol because he's the driver.

Wrap Up

■ PRONOUN CROSSWORD

Complete the following activity with a partner. Discuss your answers.

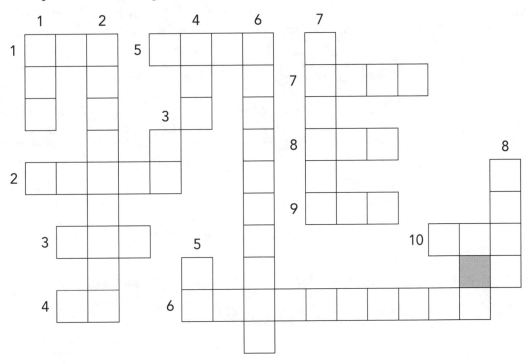

Across

1. Margaret visits … father in Mexico each winter.
2. … are many mountains in British Columbia.
3. Mr. Williams washes … hair every morning.
4. That is my cake. Give it to … now!
5. My friends are nice. … are also very generous.
6. Some people like solve problems by …
7. Sophie has a lot of jewelry. That ring is definitely …
8. The car lost … wheel on the highway.
9. Margaret is friendly, but … is also a bit snobby.
10. We sometimes ask … teacher for help.

Down

1. Mike lost … wallet in the subway.
2. When a pronoun reflects back on the subject, it is called a … pronoun.
3. When Gary Kasparov loses a chess game, … sometimes gets upset.
4. When Gary is angry, do not ask … to talk to you.
5. This is a great day because … is so sunny.
6. You and Charles should protect … from the sun.
7. That car isn't mine. It belongs to the Smiths. I am sure it is … (Mr. and Mrs. Smith's car).
8. That car is … (mine and Susan's).

3 Simple Present

Use this tense to refer to an action that is a habit or a fact.

EXAMPLES: *Birds have wings.* (Fact)
Mike plays baseball every summer. (Habit)

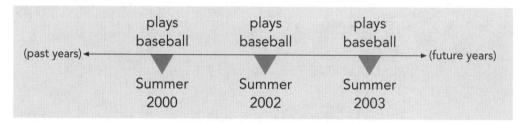

plays baseball	plays baseball	plays baseball
Summer 2000	Summer 2002	Summer 2003

(past years) ← → (future years)

Key words: always / often / usually / generally / sometimes / seldom / rarely / never / everyday - week …

AFFIRMATIVE	QUESTION FORM ADD *DO* OR *DOES*	NEGATIVE FORM ADD *DO NOT* OR *DOES NOT*	CONTRACTED FORM
I think	Do I	I do not	don't
You think	Do you	You do not	don't
She thinks	Does she	She does not	doesn't
He thinks (Add *s* or *es*)	Does he think?	He does not think.	doesn't
It thinks	Does it	It does not	doesn't
We think	Do we	We do not	don't
They think	Do they	They do not	don't

■ EXCEPTION: BE (*IS, AM, ARE*)

AFFIRMATIVE	QUESTION FORM MOVE "BE" BEFORE THE SUBJECT	NEGATIVE FORM ADD "NOT"	CONTRACTED FORM
I am	*Am I*	*I am not*	—
He / She / It is	*Is she*	*She is not*	*(isn't)*
We / You / They are	*Are they*	*They are not*	*(aren't)*

FOCUS ON THE VERB *BE*

Remember that the verb *be* is used when we want to identify:

Age   He is 40 years old. (Never use *has* to depict age!)
Hunger and thirst   Ellen is thirsty and I am hungry.
Temperature   It is very cold and rainy outside. It is never warm this time of year.

Do not use *be* to express agreement.

I ~~am~~ agree.

EXERCISE ❶ **PART A:** Make the verb negative and use the contracted form.

EXAMPLE: Jason **is** very tired. _____ *isn't*

1. The apartment building **is** sixty years old. _____

2. The main office **is** open. _____

3. Some people **are** very unhappy about the building maintenance. _____

4. I **am** happy with my apartment. _____

PART B: Write a yes/no question for each of the following sentences. Change the subject to a subject pronoun.

EXAMPLE: The furnace is too old. _____ *Is it too old?*

5. The stairwells are dirty. _____

6. Dr. Lo is the oldest tenant. _____

7. Those dogs are very old. _____

8. There is a new lock on the front door. _____

Present Tense Verbs

■ SUBJECT-VERB AGREEMENT

Conjugate the verb with *s* or *es* when the subject is third-person singular (one person, place, or thing, but not *you* or *I*).

> *Pedro **needs** a holiday. He **has** a stressful job.*

▨ Indefinite Pronouns are third-person singular

Everybody, somebody, nobody, and *anybody* (or when they end in *-one* or *-thing: everyone, everything*) are considered third-person singular nouns.

wants

EXAMPLE: Everybody ~~want~~ some coffee.

Read the following paragraph. Underline all verbs (action words) that follow third-person singular subjects. There are nine verbs to underline, not including the example.

EXAMPLE: My neighbor, Dominique Duvan, <u>loves</u> to paint landscapes.

Dominique lives in a big house just behind our house. She uses very bright colours in her artwork. Many people pay thousands of dollars for her paintings and sculptures. Everybody thinks she is a good artist. My aunt and uncle collect art. Sometimes my aunt buys Dominique's work. My aunt has a lot of money, and she loves to spend it on art. She prefers to support local artists, so she often visits Dominique's studio. I sometimes sculpt, but I am not a good artist. My brother and I sculpt in my neighbour's studio. Dominique gives us art lessons.

EXERCISE 2   Put the verb in parentheses in the simple present.

EXAMPLE: The travel agency always (open) _____ *opens* _____ on Saturdays.

1. The agent (need) _____ to reserve our airline tickets.

2. My aunt often (buy) _____ a first-class ticket.

3. Somebody (take) _____ care of my aunt's cat.

4. Trips to Costa Rica generally (cost) _____ about $1500.

5. Your flight (cost) _____ only $699.

6. We (know) _____ some people in Costa Rica.

7. The air hostess generally (meet) _____ all of the passengers.

8. Mr. Ross usually (read) _____ a magazine when he is on an airplane.

9. Sometimes Mr. and Mrs. Ross (spend) _____ time in Vancouver.

10. Everybody in my family (like) _____ Vancouver.

EXERCISE 3   Each verb is in italics. Conjugate verbs that follow third-person singular subjects. Only the verb "to be" is already conjugated correctly. There are eight verbs to conjugate, not including the example.

owns

1. My father (*own*) a car repair shop. He often *ask* me to help him. Everybody *like* my

   father. Sometimes I *help* him after school. Every weekend, on Saturday or Sunday, my sister and I **try** to help my father in the shop. My sister **ride** her mountain bike and I **take** my motorcycle. Unfortunately, my motorcycle **need** new tires.

2. The Kumars **are** very nice people. Rajiv **work** in a popular restaurant. Many university students **come** to Rajiv's place. When somebody **move** into our neighbourhood, Rajiv **greet** that person. I sometimes **think** that everybody **know** Rajiv.

THIRD-PERSON SINGULAR: SPELLING TIPS

Add *es* to verbs that end in *s*, *ch*, *sh*, *x*, and *o*.

I fix	*He fixes*
We go	*It goes*

Change *y* to *ies* when the verb ends in *consonant* + *y*.

I study	*She studies*
You carry	*He carries*

Note: if the verb ends in *vowel* + *y*, then keep the *y* and add *s*.

We play	*He plays*

Have becomes *has* in the third-person singular form.

We have	*She **has***
You have	*He **has***

EXERCISE 4   Write the third-person singular form of the following verbs.

EXAMPLE: carry _____ *carries* _____

1. hurry _____
2. fly _____
3. wish _____
4. desire _____
5. play _____

6. have _____
7. touch _____
8. wash _____
9. think _____
10. do _____

Simple Present – Negative Form

Place *do* or *does* and the word *not* between the subject and the verb.

We **<u>do not work</u>** every day. (or **don't**)
She **<u>does not work</u>** a lot. (or **doesn't**)

When the main verb is *be* (*is, am, are*) just add "not."

> *She **is not** happy.*

EXERCISE 5 Make the following verbs negative.

EXAMPLE: I go _____don't go_____

He goes _____doesn't go_____

1. We *like* _____
2. You *have* _____
3. She *has* _____
4. It *is* _____
5. Jeff *wants* _____
6. Ali *studies* _____
7. They *try* _____
8. I *hope* _____
9. Ms. Ng *lives* _____
10. We *live* _____

EXERCISE 6 **PART A:** Add *s* or *es* to the verb if necessary. (If the verb is *have*, you may have to remove the final *ve*.) Then write the negative form in the space provided.

EXAMPLE: He *drink*⁴_____ alcohol. _____doesn't drink_____

1. Ben *have*_____ a lot of bad habits. _____

2. He *smoke*_____ a pack a day. _____

3. Ben and his brother *eat*_____ a lot of greasy food. _____

4. Ben *finish*_____ a six-pack of beer every day. _____

5. They *watch*_____ TV every evening. _____

6. Ben *stay*_____ up late every night. _____

7. Ben and his brother *argue*_____ a lot. _____

PART B: Put the correct form of the verb "be" in the spaces. Then write the negative form.

EXAMPLE: Ben's dogs (be) _____are_____ well-behaved. _____are not_____

8. Ben's pit bull (be) _____ extremely dangerous. _____

9. His two Dobermans (be) _____ puppies. _____

10. The dogs (be) _____ on leashes. _____

Simple Present – Question Form

Add the auxiliary *do* or *does* to create questions. When you add *does* to the sentence, the *–s* is no longer needed on the verb.

EXAMPLE:

subject	verb		auxiliary	subject	verb
He	complains a lot.		***Does***	he	complain a lot?
They	complain a lot.		***Do***	they	complain a lot?

■ **When the main verb is *do*:**

Do is a verb, and *do* is also an auxiliary. When the main verb is *do* or *does*, you must still add an auxiliary to question and negative forms!

She always does her homework. ***Does*** she always ***do*** her homework?
                                        auxiliary   verb

EXERCISE ❼ Combine the subject and verb to create questions. Remember to add the appropriate auxiliary.

EXAMPLE: (Ben, like) _____*Does Ben like*_____ to travel?

1. (that child, have) _____ any parents?

2. (we, have) _____ time to talk?

3. (Eric, usually do) _____ the dishes?

4. (you, know) _____ the answer?

5. (somebody, want) _____ this coffee?

6. (they, do) _____ many activities?

7. (your sister, believe) _____ in ghosts?

Note: When the main verb is *be*, do not add *do* or *does* to question forms. Simply move *be* before the subject of the sentence.

EXAMPLE: (you, be) _____*Are you*_____ hungry?

8. (anybody, be) _____ thirsty?

9. (the doctors, be) _____ ready to go?

10. (your sister, be) _____ an engineer?

Frequency Adverbs

Frequency adverbs define the frequency of an action.

never	rarely	seldom	sometimes occasionally	usually generally	often frequently	always

0% → 100%
of the time

■ Placement of frequency adverbs:

- after *be*   *She is **often** tired. He is **rarely** late.*
- before all other simple tense verbs   *He **usually** sleeps late. I **sometimes** stay up late.*
- between two-part verbs   *She can **always** help us.*
- after the subject in question forms   *Does she **occasionally** sleep late?*

EXERCISE 8   Put an arrow indicating where the frequency adverb should be placed.

<u>EXAMPLE:</u>   (sometimes)   Alan takes the bus home from work.

1. (seldom)   The landlord visits the building.

2. (often)   The workers are very tired.

3. (sometimes)   They work for sixteen-hour shifts.

4. (never)   Frank is late for work.

5. (always)   Barbara complains about the heating system.

6. (usually)   Do you love your apartment?

7. (sometimes)   Is the landlord in a bad mood?

8. (always)   Does Mr. Gill get a lot of exercise?

Take Another Look

Ask yourself the following questions. If you don't know an answer, go back and review the appropriate section.

1. Circle the key words that indicate when you should use the simple present tense.

   everyday   right now   sometimes   yesterday   often   always

2. When do you put an *s* or *es* on verbs?

   _____

3. What are the question and negative forms of the following sentences?

   a) Jeff is nice.

   Yes/No question form   _____

   Negative form   _____

   b) He often studies.

   Yes/No question form   _____

   Negative form   _____

   c) They live together.

   Yes/No question form   _____

   Negative form   _____

CLASS EXERCISE (REVIEW)

PART A: Write the present-tense form of the verb in parentheses, and then write the negative form in the space provided.

EXAMPLE: Chandra (have) _____*has*_____ daily siestas. _____*doesn't have*_____

1. Mr. and Mrs. Santana (live) _____ in New Mexico.   _____

2. They (have) _____ three children.   _____

3. They (be) _____ very happy together.   _____

4. Maggie (study) _____ yoga.   _____

5. Carlos (have) _____ a good job.   _____

PART B: Make yes / no questions out of the following sentences.

<u>EXAMPLE:</u>　　He works alone

Does he work alone?

6. Carlos loves to travel.

_____

7. They fly to Mexico every year.

_____

8. His wife works in Toronto.

_____

9. They travel a lot.

_____

10. She takes a vacation every winter.

_____

Wrap Up

■ TALK ABOUT SCHEDULES

Find a partner. Interview your partner. What is your partner's schedule? Ask your partner when he or she does the following activities.

Remember to write the time like this: 10:00 or 10 AM.

	WEEKDAYS					WEEKENDS	
	Monday	Tuesday	Wednesday	Thursday	Friday	Saturday	Sunday
Wake up							
Go to classes							
Eat lunch							
Study							
Watch TV							
Go to bed							

4 Present Progressive

UNIT

Present Progressive (now)

1. Indicates that an action is happening now.

2. Indicates that an action is happening for a present, temporary period of time.

Key words: now, at this moment, currently, these days…

AFFIRMATIVE		QUESTION FORM MOVE *BE* BEFORE THE SUBJECT		NEGATIVE FORM ADD *NOT*	
I am		**Am** I		I am	
You are		**Are** you		You are	
She is		**Is** she		She is	
He is	sleeping.	**Is** he	sleeping?	He is	**not** sleeping.
It is		**Is** it		It is	
We are		**Are** we		We are	
They are		**Are** they		They are	

CLASS EXERCISE

Identify all examples of the present progressive by circling *be* and the *-ing* form of the verb. There are ten present progressive verbs in the paragraph, not including the example.

I (am sitting) in a chai shop in a village in Bengal, India. Chai means "tea." A small man is cooking the chai in a large pot on the stove. The milk, tea, and sugar are boiling in the pot. I want to drink my tea without sugar, but it is not possible. In India, many people cook tea with milk and sugar in it. Now the man is stirring the tea.

A woman is sitting at the next table. She is wearing orange clothing. She has two children, and her children are arguing about something. At another table, an old man is reading a newspaper and he is drinking a cup of chai. The old man is wearing a baggy white shirt and white pants. I am enjoying the aroma of the chai. The chai contains the spice cardamom, and it smells wonderful.

■ SPELLING TIP: -ING VERB FORMS

LAST LETTER(S) OF VERB	EXAMPLE	"-ING" FORM	RULE
silent *e*	*smile*	*smiling*	delete the *e*, add *-ing*
y	*fly, play*	*flying, playing*	just add *-ing*
ie	*lie*	*lying*	change the *ie* to *y* and add *-ing*.
one vowel-one consonant	*stop*	*stopping*	double the last letter (exception: words that end in *X* or *W*. snow – snowing, fix – fixing)

EXERCISE ❶ Write the following verbs in their *-ing* form. Refer to the preceding chart for rules.

EXAMPLE: try _____*trying*_____

1. hope _____

2. marry _____

3. think _____

4. run _____

5. study _____

6. shop _____

7. sit _____

8. buy _____

9. plan _____

10. write _____

11. rain _____

12. sing _____

Present Progressive: Question and Negative Forms

Question: The verb *be* acts as an auxiliary and goes before the subject.

Ray is cooking dinner. *Why is Ray cooking dinner?*

Negative: Place *not* after the verb *be*. *Ray isn't cooking dinner.*

EXERCISE ❷

Read the description. Write what the person is doing. Then write a yes/no question. Use one of the following verbs.

whistle	sneeze	cough	scratch
~~laugh~~	cry	snore	yawn

EXAMPLE:

Sentence

Question

She is laughing.

Is she laughing?

1. _____

_____

2. _____

_____

3. _____

_____

4. _____

_____

5. _____

_____

6. _____

_____

EXERCISE ③ Put the verb in the present progressive form. Then make the sentences negative. (Use the contracted form.)

EXAMPLE:　Helena (sing) ___*is singing*___ a beautiful song. ___*isn't singing.*___

1. Vincent (direct) _____ the movie. _____

2. Helena (act) _____. _____

3. The actors (rest) _____. _____

4. The cameraman (film) _____ a scene. _____

5. The caterers (prepare) _____ lunch. _____

6. Helena (wait) _____ in her dressing room. _____

Comparing the Simple Present and the Present Progressive

EXERCISE ④ Conjugate the verbs in parenthesis to make a simple present or present progressive sentence. If the action is a fact or a habit, use the simple present tense. If the action is happening now, use the present progressive (*ing*) tense. After each sentence, write:

　H　　if the action is a habit
　F　　if it is a fact
　N　　if the action is happening now.

EXAMPLE:　　Look! That man (steal) your car!　　___*is stealing (N)*___

1. Leo usually (travel) to Chile in July and August. _____

2. Leo (visit) his family at this moment. _____

3. Leo's father (own) a restaurant in Santiago. _____

4. Mr. Cruz (serve) customers right now. _____

5. Look! Leo's brother, Pilo, (dance) alone. _____

6. Mrs. Cruz (want) Leo to move back to Chile. _____

7. Mrs. Cruz and Leo (discuss) the issue at this moment. _____

8. Leo's sister often (complain) about Chile's government. _____

9. In fact, she (complain) right now. _____

Non-Progressive Verbs

Sometimes we cannot use progressive verb forms. The following verbs are generally not used in the progressive tense.

EXAMPLE: I am ~~know~~ing you.   *know*

PERCEPTION	PREFERENCE OR STATE		POSSESSION
see	like	know	own
hear	hate	understand	have (meaning "possess")
smell	want	recognize	possess
taste	prefer	believe	belong
feel	need	think (meaning "in my opinion")	

EXERCISE 5   Complete the sentences using the simple present or the present progressive.

EXAMPLE: Mark (like) _____ *likes* _____ cake. He (eat)

_____ *is eating* _____ a piece of cake right now.

1. I (love) _____ to travel. Right now I (visit)

_____ Istanbul. There (be) _____

many people in the streets. I (sit) _____ near the steps

of the Blue Mosque. It (rain) _____ very lightly, but

I (be) _____ dry, because I (hold) _____

an umbrella over my head.

2. In Turkey, people generally (put, not) _____ milk in

their coffee. My boyfriend (hate) _____ strong coffee.

Right now, in his backpack, he (carry) _____ a jar

of instant coffee. I (think) _____ that instant coffee

(taste) _____ terrible. Now my boyfriend and I (relax)

_____ .

EXERCISE 6   Beside each sentence write the yes/no question and negative forms. Change the subject to a subject pronoun.

EXAMPLES: Jay shops every day.   Ray is sleeping now.

Question: _*Does he shop every day?*_   Question: _*Is he sleeping now?*_

Negative: _*He doesn't shop every day.*_   Negative: _*He isn't sleeping now.*_

1. Sandra is staying in a hotel this weekend.

   Question: _____

   Negative: _____

2. Joe and Carlos are roommates.

   Question: _____

   Negative: _____

3. They pay $600 a month in rent.

   Question form: _____

   Negative form: _____

4. Carlos has a busy life.

   Question: _____

   Negative: _____

5. Carlos is sleeping on the sofa now.

   Question: _____

   Negative: _____

Question Words

QUESTION WORD	REFERS TO:	QUESTION WORD	REFERS TO:
Who	a person *Who won the award?* *Who(m)* did you call?*	**How**	a method or degree *How cold is it?*
What	a thing *What is your name?*	**How long**	a period of time *How long is the movie?*
When	a time *When does the show start?*	**How far**	a distance *How far is Laval from here?*
Where	a place *Where do you live?*	**How often**	frequency of activity *How often do you see a dentist?*
Why	a reason *Why is he late?*	**How much / How many**	amount of something *How much does it cost?* *How many dogs do you have?*

*Whom is used in formal English. You will not be expected to use *whom* in this course.

EXERCISE 7 Write the question in the space provided. The exact answer to the question is in bold.

EXAMPLE: Ellen keeps her keys **in her purse**. _____Where does she keep her keys?_____

1. Birds have hollow bones **because it helps them fly**.

   _____

2. Owls sleep **during the day**.

   _____

3. They hunt **for several hours** each night.

   _____

4. Monica works **in an animal shelter**.

   _____

5. She is bringing **a parrot** to the clinic right now.

   _____

6. Monica works with **Mr. Bakar**.

   _____

7. Mr. Bakar is **cleaning the cages**.

   _____

8. There are **fifty** cages in the shelter.

   _____

EXERCISE 8 Correct the errors in verb tense or verb form in the following paragraphs. There are fifteen underlined errors.

EXAMPLE:

                                                       looks

    Every year, on July 1, Martin is ~~looking~~ for a new apartment.

In most cities, apartments are for rent all year, but in Quebec, Canada, there is

a special moving day. Every July 1, thousands of people <u>moves</u> from one place

to another. Moving companies <u>are charging</u> a high price every June and July.

Right now Todd and Carlos <u>is looking</u> for an apartment. They <u>are walk</u> down Duluth

Street and they <u>trying</u> to find a place to live. Carlos <u>holding</u> a newspaper and Todd

<u>is makes</u> a call on his cell phone.

This year, landlords <u>are knowing</u> that there <u>is</u> not a lot of apartments available. Right now some landlords <u>are exploit</u> the situation by raising their rents a lot. For example, the apartments <u>is</u> very expensive in the area near Jeanne Mance Park. Mr. Lebrun <u>haves</u> a building near the park, and he <u>want</u> $1500 for a two-bedroom apartment. Todd and Carlos <u>have not</u> enough money to pay such a high rent. Todd <u>don't has</u> a job and Carlos earns a very low salary.

Take Another Look

Answer the following questions. If you don't know an answer, then go back and review the appropriate section!

1. Which key words indicate that you should use the present progressive tense?

   everyday   now   sometimes   at this moment   yesterday

2. What is the difference between the two following sentences?

   Adela sings every day. _____

   Adela is singing right now. _____

3. What are the question and negative forms of the following sentences?

   a) She is working.

   Yes/No question form _____

   Negative form _____

   b) He eats meat.

   Yes/No question form _____

   Negative form _____

   c) They eat meat.

   Yes/No question form _____

   Negative form _____

   d) They are reading.

   Yes/No question form _____

   Negative form _____

CLASS EXERCISE (REVIEW)

PART A: Combine the words in parenthesis to make a simple present or present progressive sentence.

Mr. Martin (work, not) during the summer months. _____ *doesn't work*

The nurse (examine) the patient right now. _____ *is examining*

1. Right now Anne (sit) in an airplane. _____

2. Anne's husband often (smoke). _____

3. At the moment he (smoke, not) a cigarette. _____

4. The pilot usually (like) his job. _____

5. Some students in the front row (study)
   for their exam right now. _____

6. The plane usually (go, not) over Greenland. _____

7. The flight attendants (serve) dinner right now. _____

PART B: Create questions. The answers to the questions are in bold.

8. The plane is going **to England**.

   _____

9. He usually visits England **in the spring**.

   _____

10. The passengers are waiting **in the next room**.

    _____

11. Those cups have **tea** in them.

    _____

Wrap Up

■ DESCRIBE THE MOMENT

Look at the following pictures. With a partner, write a paragraph about each picture. Explain what is happening now. Example: *The woman in a white coat is drinking coffee.* You will need your dictionary for this activity.

Before you write: Do you know the meaning of the following verbs?

spill	drop	steal	sniff
wipe	crawl	scream	kiss

A _____

_____

_____

_____

_____

_____

_____

_____

5 Simple Past

Use the simple past to indicate that an action was completed at a definite time in the past.

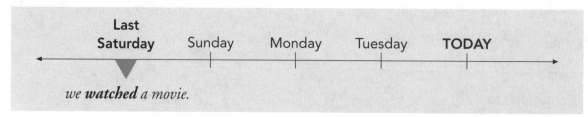

| | Last Saturday | Sunday | Monday | Tuesday | TODAY |

*we **watched** a movie.*

Key words: ago, yesterday, last week, last month, last year, five years ago, when I was a child…

AFFIRMATIVE	QUESTION FORM ADD *DID*	NEGATIVE FORM ADD *DID NOT*
I He She It You We They } slept.	Did I he she it you we they } sleep?	I He She It You We They } **did not** sleep. (didn't)

Be

AFFIRMATIVE	QUESTION FORM MOVE POSITION OF *BE*	NEGATIVE FORM ADD *NOT*
I He She It } was ready.	Was I he she it } ready?	I He She It } was **not** ready. (wasn't)
You We They } were late.	Were you we they } late?	You We They } were **not** late. (weren't)

■ FOCUS ON THE VERB *BE*

EXERCISE ①   **PART A:** Read the following sentences about Marilyn Monroe. Write *was* or *were* in the spaces provided.

EXAMPLE: In the 1950s, many men _____*were*_____ in love with Marilyn Monroe.

1. Marilyn Monroe _____ born on June 1, 1926, in the Los Angeles General Hospital.

2. When _____ you born?

3. In the 1920's, Marilyn's mother _____ a film-cutter at RKO films.

4. Marilyn Monroe _____ a very lonely child because her mother _____ often ill.

5. Marilyn and her mother _____ very unhappy.

6. Many people _____ surprised when Marilyn Monroe became a movie star.

PART B: Make the verbs in the following sentences negative. Use the contracted negative form.

EXAMPLE: Marilyn's first film *was* in 1949.   _____*wasn't*_____

7. In the 1950s, Marilyn *was* in many great films.   _____

8. John and Robert Kennedy *were* close friends of Marilyn. _____

9. Many people believe that Marilyn *was* JFK's lover.   _____

10. Some people *were* sad when Marilyn died.   _____

EXERCISE ②   Note the differences between *there was* and *there were*:

There **was** (one thing)   There **were** (two or more things)

Put *There was* or *There were* in the space provided. Then write a yes/no question by putting *Was there* or *Were there* in the space provided.

EXAMPLE: _____*There was*_____ a fire yesterday.

Question: _____*Was there*_____ a fire yesterday?

1. _____ too many people in the line up last night.

Question: Why _____ too many people in the line up last night?

2. _____ a big storm last night.

Question: _____ a big storm last night?

3. _____ a robbery at 10 PM.

    Question: Why _____ a robbery at 10 PM?

4. _____ three policemen on our street yesterday.

    Question: Why _____ three police officers on our street yesterday?

EXERCISE 3   Read the following sentences about Marilyn Monroe. Turn the sentences into questions. The answer to each question is in bold.

EXAMPLE: Marilyn's first film was *The Shocking Miss Pilgrim*.

       What was her first film?

1. **Yes**, Marilyn was a good actress.

    _____

2. Her first film was **in 1947**.

    _____

3. Her salary was **$125** per week.

    _____

4. Many people were nice to Marilyn **because she was so beautiful**.

    _____

5. **Yes**, Arthur Miller was a very good writer.

    _____

6. He was Marilyn's husband **in the mid-1950s**.

    _____

7. **Yes**, their marriage was short.

    _____

8. Many actors were angry with Marilyn **because she was usually late for work**.

    _____

9. **Yes**, some of her films were good.

    _____

10. She was single **in 1962**.

    _____

Regular Past-Tense Verbs

There are both regular and irregular past tense verbs. Regular verbs take *-ed* and generally do not appear on verb lists, such as the one at the back of this book, because of their standard form.

> **SPELLING OF REGULAR (*ED*) PAST TENSE VERBS**
>
> 1. Double the <u>last</u> letter of one-syllable verbs that end in a consonant-vowel-consonant combination.
>
>   stop - *stopped*   jog - *jogged*
>
> 2. When verbs end in *consonant-y*, change the *y* to *i* and add *ed*.
>
>   fry - *fried*   apply - *applied*
>
>   When verbs end in *vowel-y*, usually keep the *y*.
>
>   play - *played*   *Exception: pay - *paid*

EXERCISE 4   Write the *-ed* form of these regular verbs.

EXAMPLE: stop _____*stopped*_____

1. carry _____
2. stay _____
3. rely _____
4. marry _____
5. share _____
6. rain _____
7. fail _____
8. slap _____

9. hope _____
10. wash _____
11. remain _____
12. study _____
13. plan _____
14. try _____
15. shop _____

■ PAST TENSE – QUESTION FORM

Add *did*, and use the base form of the verb.

James **married** Marilyn.   **Did** he **marry** her?
                                     When **did** he **marry** her?

Exception: the verbs *was* and *were*   She was late. Was she late?

EXERCISE **5**   Write the past form of each verb. Then write a yes/no question.

EXAMPLE: John Lennon (marry) _____*married*_____ Yoko Ono.

Did John Lennon marry Yoko Ono?

In the 1970s,

1. John and Yoko (live) _____ in New York.

Question: _____

2. They (work) _____ together.

Question: _____

3. They (separate) _____ for two years.

Question: _____

4. John (call) _____ their separation "the lost weekend."

Question: _____

5. Yoko (create) _____ many short films.

Question: _____

6. The FBI (investigate) _____ John.

Question: _____

Irregular Past Tense Verbs

CLASS EXERCISE

Do you know the past form of these irregular verbs? Put the past tense form in the spaces provided. Do as many as you can. If you need help, check the irregular verb list in the appendix.

1. be _____*was, were*_____   **8.** cost _____

2. become _____   **9.** cut _____

3. begin _____   **10.** do _____

4. break _____   **11.** drink _____

5. bring _____   **12.** drive _____

6. buy _____   **13.** eat _____

7. choose _____   **14.** fall _____

15. feel _____   23. leave _____

16. find _____   24. lose _____

17. get _____   25. make _____

18. give _____   26. ride _____

19. go _____   27. sing _____

20. have _____   28. speak _____

21. hear _____   29. take _____

22. know _____   30. think _____

EXERCISE 6 **PART A:** Fill in the blanks with the appropriate simple past form. The verb may be a regular or an irregular verb.

1. Muhammad Ali was born in 1942 and he (begin) _____*began*_____ to box
   at the age of twelve. He (become) _____ a great boxer in the
   1960s. He (fight) _____ against Joe Frazier in 1970 in "The Fight
   of the Century." He (win) _____ the fight. Many people (admire)
   _____ him. Many companies (want) _____
   to hire Ali for advertising, but Ali (refuse) _____ to advertise
   for companies.

2. Jackie Robinson (start) _____ to play baseball in the early 1940s.
   He (play) _____ for the Montreal Royals team and then he (join)
   _____ the Brooklyn Dodgers in 1947. He (break) _____
   the colour-barrier in major-league baseball.

3. Mr. Woods (go) _____ to Vietnam during the Vietnam War.
   He (meet) _____ a man called Tiger. Tiger (die) _____
   during the war. Later, in the 1970s, Mr. Woods (name) _____ his
   son Tiger to honour his friend. Tiger Woods (hit) _____ his first
   golf ball when he was only two years old. At age 15, Tiger Woods (be) _____
   the youngest golfer to win the U.S. Amateur Championship.

PART B: Now look again at Part A. Put the verbs in parentheses into the following columns. There are eight regular verbs, and nine irregular verbs. The first ones are done for you.

REGULAR VERBS	IRREGULAR VERBS
1. _____ admired _____	1. _____ began _____
2. _____	2. _____
3. _____	3. _____
4. _____	4. _____
5. _____	5. _____
6. _____	6. _____
7. _____	7. _____
8. _____	8. _____
	9. _____

PAST TENSE: REVIEW QUESTION AND NEGATIVE FORMS

Question: Add *did* to create questions. When you add *did* to the sentence, use the base form of the verb!

auxiliary

Diego met Frida in 1924.   *When* **did** *Diego* **meet** *Frida?*

Negative: Add *did not* (or *didn't*)   *Diego* **did not** (or **didn't**) *meet Frida in 1924.*

Exception (be): In questions, just move *be* before the subject.

Were you late?   *You* **were not** (or **weren't**) *late.*

EXERCISE 7   Write the negative form of the following past-tense verbs. Use the contracted forms.

EXAMPLE: I **tried**   _____ didn't try _____

Joe **was** late.   _____ wasn't _____

1. We **were** busy.   _____

2. She **wrote** it.   _____

3. I **thought** so.   _____

4. It **happened**.   _____

5. It **was** hot.   _____

6. We **brought** it.   _____

7. He **felt** good.   _____

EXERCISE 8 Put the verb in parentheses into the past form. Then make a question and negative sentence. The sentences are all about the nineteenth-century artist Paul Gauguin, so they must be in the past tense.

EXAMPLE: Paul Gauguin (live) _____ *lived* _____ in Tahiti.

Question: _*Did Paul Gauguin live in Tahiti?*_

Negative: _*Paul Gauguin didn't live in Tahiti.*_

1. Paul (be) _____ originally a banker.

Question: _____

Negative: _____

2. He (leave) _____ his family in 1887.

Question: _____

Negative: _____

3. Paul (stay) _____ with Vincent Van Gogh.

Question: _____

Negative: _____

4. They (have) _____ many arguments.

Question: _____

Negative: _____

5. They (be) _____ very passionate about art.

Question: _____

Negative: _____

EXERCISE 9 Circle the past tense error and correct it in the space provided.

EXAMPLE: Joe DiMaggio didn't (played) football. _____ *play* _____

1. Did Joe DiMaggio was a great baseball player? _____

2. When did Marilyn moved to Hollywood? _____

3. Marilyn maked many movies. _____

4. Joe did'nt like Marilyn's movies. _____

5. You was late for the movie yesterday. _____

6. You did not watched the movie with me. _____

7. When I was young, I was have a hero. _____

8. I did like to see my hero on television. _____

9. My sister don't really had a hero. _____

10. My hero were an example for me. _____

Take Another Look

Ask yourself the following questions. If you don't know an answer, go back and check that section.

1. Which key words indicate that you need the simple past tense?

   sometimes   yesterday   last week   next Friday   now   two days ago

2. Write the past form of: **a)** *is* _____   **b)** *are* _____

3. What are the question and negative forms of the following past-tense sentences?

a) She was nasty.

   Yes/No question form   _____

   Negative form   _____

b) We were late.

   Yes/No question form   _____

   Negative form   _____

c) They cleaned it.

   Yes/No question form   _____

   Negative form   _____

d) She ate lunch.

   Yes/No question form   _____

   Negative form   _____

CLASS EXERCISE (REVIEW)

PART A: Write the correct past form of the verb in parenthesis. The sentences are all about Marilyn Monroe, so they must be in the past tense.

EXAMPLE: Marilyn (live, not) in New York. _____ *didn't live* _____

1. Marilyn Monroe (know, not) her father. _____

2. She (have) several husbands. _____

3. Marilyn (finish, not) high school. _____

4. She (fall) off a horse when she was 27. _____

5. Some people (respect, not) Marilyn's work. _____

PART B: Make yes/no questions. The answers are in italics.

<u>EXAMPLE:</u>   Marilyn met her first husband *in an airplane factory*.

Where did Marilyn meet her first husband? _____

6. James married her *in 1942*.

_____

7. Marilyn was *16 years old* when she got married.

_____

8. She stayed with James *for four years*.

_____

9. The Marx Brothers wanted Marilyn in their movie *because they liked her*.

_____

10. *Yes*, they were happy with her performance.

_____

Wrap Up

■ IRREGULAR VERB PUZZLE

Circle the past tense forms of the following verbs. Words may be written in any direction (upside down, sideways, diagonally). Then write the past form beside the verb.

W	A	D	R	A	N	K	F	E	L	T	V	L
E	W	R	O	T	E	P	G	H	M	I	U	O
N	B	E	C	A	M	E	M	A	D	E	J	S
T	B	T	A	U	G	H	T	M	V	X	C	T
A	O	D	B	R	O	K	E	E	S	E	H	W
S	T	I	M	R	D	P	B	T	P	K	O	T
S	A	D	R	G	R	D	E	D	E	N	S	H
C	C	I	L	C	O	C	G	K	N	E	E	O
U	F	M	D	I	V	T	A	H	T	W	I	U
T	E	E	H	G	E	K	N	Z	A	D	K	G
O	O	N	L	B	L	E	F	T	U	D	S	H
L	F	O	S	L	Z	S	P	O	K	E	P	T
D	G	S	K	A	T	E	B	O	U	G	H	T

become	have
begin	know
break	leave
buy	lose
choose	make
cut	meet
do	say
drink	speak
~~drive~~ *drove*	spend
eat	take
fall	teach
feel	tell
get	think
give	write
go	

6 Past Progressive

Use the past progressive to:

1. indicate that an action was in progress at an understood or stated past time.

At 3:30 AM	Now

*we **were sleeping**.*

2. indicate that an action was in progress when another action interrupted it.

The fire started	Now

*when we **were sleeping**.*

3. describe two actions that were continuing at the same time.

EXAMPLE: *Yesterday, while **I was setting** the table, my sister **was resting** on the sofa.*

Don't forget that some verbs, such as *understand*, are non-progressive. The chart of non-progressive verbs is in **Unit 4**, on page 29.

Key words: while, as

AFFIRMATIVE	QUESTION FORM MOVE *BE* BEFORE THE SUBJECT	NEGATIVE FORM ADD *NOT*
I He She It } was sleeping.	**Was** I he she it } sleeping?	I He She It } was not sleeping. (wasn't)
You We They } were sleeping.	**Were** you we they } sleeping?	You We They } were not sleeping. (weren't)

EXERCISE ❶ Write the negative past progressive form of the following verbs.

EXAMPLE: Carl (study) _____*wasn't studying*_____ at 6 AM.

1. You (work) _____ when I called.

2. Anne (sleep) _____ last night at midnight.

3. Jane and Michael _____ (walk) the dog when the murder happened.

4. The doctor (examining) _____ the patient when I entered the office.

5. Remi and I (discuss) _____ the problem when you interrupted us.

6. The couple behind me (talk) _____ during the movie last night.

CLASS EXERCISE

Read the pairs of sentences and then answer the question that follows.

1. Diego was laughing during the movie.
Uri laughed once during the movie.

Who thought the movie was really funny? _____

2. When the movie ended Diego left the theater.
When the movie ended Uri was leaving the theater.

Who didn't watch the end of the movie? _____

3. Later, while Diego was making spaghetti, he heard the baby cry.
Later, while Uri was making spaghetti, the baby was crying.

Which man ignored the crying baby? _____

EXERCISE ❷ Fill in the blanks with the simple past or the past progressive tense.

The Robbery

EXAMPLE: Somebody (enter) _____ *entered* _____ a house on Mulholland Drive while the occupants (sleep) _____ *were sleeping* _____.

1. On March 1st, at 1 AM, I (sleep) _____ when the crime happened. I (hear, not) _____ a thing.

2. In the night, while we (dream) _____, a robber entered the house. The robber (take) _____ our television and computer.

3. The next morning, I (call) _____ the police. Then I (sit) _____ down and I (eat) _____ breakfast.

4. The police inspector (arrive) _____ while we (eat)

   _____ breakfast.

5. While my brother and I (talk) _____ with the police

   officer, the officer's cellphone (ring) _____. The officer

   (interrupt) _____ us and then he (answer) _____

   his phone. He (talk) _____ for a few minutes and then he (tell)

   _____ us that he had to leave.

6. One month later, on April 1st, the police (find) _____

   our television, but they (find, not) _____ our computer.

PAST PROGRESSIVE TIPS

Do not use the past progressive to talk about past habits.

       wrote
    He ~~was writing~~ music when he was younger.

Do not use the past progressive to describe a series of past actions.

         played   *went*
    When I was a child, I ~~was playing~~ baseball. Every night I ~~was going~~ to the field
    to practice my batting...

Do not overuse the past progressive! Only use this tense to emphasize that a past action *was in progress.*

EXERCISE 3   Circle and correct the error in the following sentences. If the sentence is correct, write C in the space.

    <u>EXAMPLE:</u>
                                         walking
    Last week, while Martin was ~~walk~~ to work, he met an old friend. _____

1. When I was a small child, I was walking to school everyday. _____ I was always

   walked alone. _____ It was a very long walk. _____ I wasn't wanting to walk,

   but I had no choice. _____

2. One day, while I was crossing a street, a bus almost hit me. _____ The driver tried

   to avoid me and he hit a street sign. _____ It was my fault because when the

   accident happened, I wasn't pay attention to the road. _____ The driver was very

---

angry and he was yelling at me. _____ After that I was trying to be more careful.

_____ I was always looked in both directions at street corners. _____

Present and Past Tense Review

EXERCISE 4 Look at the following sentences carefully. In each sentence, circle the auxiliary (helping verb) and underline the main verb. Sometimes with the verb *be*, there is no main verb.

<u>EXAMPLE:</u>   When (does) Anne usually <u>eat</u> dinner?

1. Why did Henry VIII divorce Catherine?

2. Was he a madman?

3. How long did Henry rule England?

4. What is your opinion about the monarchy?

5. What political party do you support?

6. What were you doing on election night?

7. How many ministers are in Ottawa?

8. What is that politician saying now?

9. Who was the best leader in the world?

10. How often does he read newspapers?

EXERCISE 5 Convert each sentence into its question and negative form. You can change the subject to a subject pronoun.

<u>EXAMPLE:</u>   Julie is working today.

Question: _*Is she working today?*_

Negative: _*She isn't working today.*_

1. Mike Myers is making a movie.

   Question: _____

   Negative: _____

2. He works in Los Angeles.

   Question: _____

   Negative: _____

3. His wife visited the movie set yesterday.

Question: _____

Negative: _____

4. Mike was filming a scene at 3 PM yesterday.

Question: _____

Negative: _____

EXERCISE 6   Create questions from the answers provided. The exact answer is in bold. Change the subject to a subject pronoun.

Question word(s)	Auxiliary	Subject	Verb ...

EXAMPLE: Mark received **a traffic ticket**. | *What* | *did* | *he* | *receive?* |

1. Mark drinks beer **every Friday**.

_____

2. He called his lawyer **because he has a legal problem**.

_____

3. The lawyer was late **last Monday**.

_____

4. The meeting lasted **for three hours**.

_____

5. Mark is **20 years** old.

_____

6. He was driving **on Highway 12** when the police stopped him.

_____

Take Another Look

Answer the following questions. If you don't know an answer, then go back and review the appropriate section!

1. When do you use the past progressive tense?

_____

2. What are the question and negative forms of the following sentences?

a) She works alone.

Yes/No question form _____

Negative form _____

b) She is working now.

Yes/No question form _____

Negative form _____

c) She was at home.

Yes/No question form _____

Negative form _____

d) She ate dinner.

Yes/No question form _____

Negative form _____

e) She was watching TV.

Yes/No question form _____

Negative form _____

CLASS EXERCISE (REVIEW)

PART A: Each sentence has one verb tense error. Circle and correct the error.

EXAMPLE: In the 1500s, Henry VIII (was ruling) England. _____ *ruled* _____

1. Henry VIII was having a very self-indulgent life. _____

2. Many of Henry's wives were losing their heads. _____

3. In 1510, while Henry was rule England, he met Catherine. _____

4. We were discussing Henry VIII when Melanie suddenly was leaving the room. _____

5. What you were doing last night at 8 PM? _____

PART B: Read these sentences about the Beatles. Put the verb in the appropriate tense. Use the simple past or past progressive.

6. One day while John (drink) _____ in a pub, he met a boy named Paul.

7. In 1960, in the city of Hamburg, the Beatles (make) _____ many shows.

8. While George (sing) _____ on a stage, he saw Patti in the audience.

9. While John (play) _____ the guitar, he suddenly fell off the stage.

10. The Beatles (visit) _____ America in 1964.

Wrap Up

■ THINK ABOUT THE PAST

Sit with a partner or a small group of students. Ask and answer the following questions.

1. What were you doing at 6 o'clock this morning?

2. What were you doing at midnight, last New Year's Eve?

3. On September 11, 2001, while terrorists were attacking New York, what were you doing?

4. How did you hear about the terrorist attacks?

5. What did you do on September 11 after you heard about the terrorist attacks?

6. How did you celebrate New Year's Eve, 2000?

7. What is your oldest childhood memory? Describe that memory.

Review of Units 1 to 6

Pronouns

CLASS EXERCISE A

Circle the correct pronouns.

EXAMPLE: Mr. Riffo lives with ((his)/ her) sister.

1. Carolyn loves to travel. Last year, she bought a backpack and she filled (her / it) with (her / his / its) clothing, books, and other supplies. Then she asked (my / me) to take a trip with her. I quit (me / my) job and I joined (she / her / hers) on a trip to Malaysia.

2. We arrived in Kuala Lumpur at 10 PM. As soon as we arrived, I lost (me / my) wallet but Carolyn didn't lose (her / hers). (Us / Our / We) got into a small taxi and went to a hotel. The hotel owners, Mr. and Mrs. Rahim, asked us to pay for (ours / our) room in advance. Carolyn paid for (it / its / they), and I promised that I would pay (her / hers) back as soon as I got some more money.

3. Mr. and Mrs. Rahim cooked really good food in (their / theirs / they) hotel kitchen. Mr. Rahim made (we / our / us) laugh with (he's / his) sense of humour. We really enjoyed (ours / us / ourselves).

The Simple Present Tense / There is, There are

CLASS EXERCISE B

Circle the letter of the best answer.

EXAMPLE: She … very hungry.
a) have   b) has   c) are   (d)) is

1. The kids … in school today.
    a) are'nt   b) isn't   c) aren't   d) is not

2. I'm sorry, but I … agree with Julie.
    a) am   b) (nothing)   c) is   d) are

3. My brother … fourteen years old.
    a) have   b) has   c) are   d) is

4. ... any children?

    a) Do she have   **b)** Does she has   **c)** Does she have   **d)** Has she

5. Why ... so tired?

    a) are you   **b)** you are   **c)** do you are   **d)** your

6. ... too many people in the restaurant.

    a) There is   **b)** It is   **c)** There are   **d)** There has

7. When ...?

    a) does class finish **b)** class finishes   **c)** do class finishes **d)** does class finishes

8. Mrs. Graham ... a nice office.

    a) haves   **b)** has   **c)** have   **d)** is

9. My mother ... to watch television.

    a) likes not   **b)** doesn't likes   **c)** don't likes   **d)** doesn't like

10. ... many mountains in Nepal?

    a) Is there   **b)** There are   **c)** Are there   **d)** Has there

The Simple Present Tense

CLASS EXERCISE C

Conjugate the verb that is in parentheses. Then make a negative statement and a question. Change the subject to a subject pronoun.

EXAMPLE: Alice (smoke) _____ *smokes* _____ .

negative: *She does not smoke.* _____

question: *Does she smoke?* _____

1. Many people (have) _____ insomnia.

negative: _____

question: _____

2. Jane (sleep) _____ six hours per night.

negative: _____

question: _____

3. Jane (be) _____ tired every day.

negative: _____

question: _____

4. Dr. Lee (work) _____ in a clinic.

negative: _____

question: _____

5. Some people (need) _____ daily naps.

negative: _____

question: _____

Information Question Words

CLASS EXERCISE D

Put the correct question word in the space provided.

who	where	how long	how many
what	why	how often	how much
when	how	how far	how old

EXAMPLE: We went to **Paris**.   _____*Where*_____

1. I went to bed **at 11 PM**.   _____

2. He is sleeping **because he is tired**.   _____

3. I talked to **Mr. Jones**.   _____

4. We ate **in a restaurant**.   _____

5. It's a **duck**.   _____

6. It costs **$300**.   _____

7. I did it **with a hammer**.   _____

8. I visit him **twice a year**.   _____

9. He is **17 years old**.   _____

10. It is **12 miles** from here.   _____

11. There are **100 people**.   _____

12. We went there **for three weeks**.   _____

Present and Simple Past Tenses: Question/Negative Forms

CLASS EXERCISE E

Fill in the blanks using the correct tense of the verb. Then write a yes/no question and a negative statement. The sentences may be in the present, present progressive, or past tenses.

<u>EXAMPLE:</u>   Chelsea (be) _____*is*_____ from England. (simple present)

Question: _*Is Chelsea from England?*_____

Negative: _*Chelsea isn't from England.*_____

1. Chelsea (speak) _____ four languages.

   Question: _____

   Negative: _____

2. She (play) _____ the piano right now.

   Question: _____

   Negative: _____

3. Chopin (write) _____ music in the 1830s.

   Question: _____

   Negative: _____

4. Chopin (be) _____ a musical genius.

   Question: _____

   Negative: _____

5. There (be) _____ many great composers in the 1800s.

   Question: _____

   Negative: _____

7 Plurals and Articles

Plural Forms

	Singular	Plural
• Most plural nouns simply have an *s* ending.	cat	*cats*
• Add *es* to nouns ending in *s*, *ch*, *sh*, *x* or *z*.	fax	*faxes*
	church	*churches*
• For most nouns ending in *f*, the *f* changes to *ves* in the plural form.	life	*lives*
	knife	*knives*
• When nouns end in consonant + *y*, change the *y* to *ies* in the plural form.	factory	*factories*
	body	*bodies*

■ IRREGULAR PLURALS

• Some nouns have irregular plural forms. These irregular forms do not need an additional *s*!

man	*men*	foot	*feet*	deer	*deer*
woman	*women*	tooth	*teeth*	sheep	*sheep*
person	*people*	fish	*fish*		
mouse	*mice*	child	*children*		

EXERCISE 1 Write the plural form of the following nouns.

EXAMPLE: man _____*men*_____

1. woman _____
2. child _____
3. fish _____
4. brush _____
5. leaf _____
6. company _____

7. knife _____
8. person _____
9. boy _____
10. fly _____
11. dish _____
12. tooth _____

Adjectives have no plural form. (Adjectives give information about nouns.)

INCORRECT: *Those are simples exercises.*
CORRECT: *Those are **simple** exercises.*

EXERCISE ❷   If the sentence is correct, write *C* in the space provided. If the sentence has an error in plural forms, correct it in the space provided.

EXAMPLE: Karen has many (nices) friends.   _____*nice*_____

1. Some people like to watch musics videos.   _____

2. There are some greats bands on television.   _____

3. Today many womens play music.   _____

4. My sister's favourite singer has blues eyes.   _____

5. Sara knows many things about her favorite singer.   _____

6. My parents are very practicals.   _____

7. They say that childrens need to read more often.   _____

8. We can't watch television on weeks days.   _____

9. Many peoples in my school watch television every day. _____

THIS / THAT / THESE / THOSE

This and *these* are used to refer to people and things that are physically close to the speaker in time or place. *That* and *those* are used to refer to things that are physically distant from the speaker in time or place.

	NEAR THE SPEAKER		FAR FROM THE SPEAKER	
Singular	**this**	*This is my shirt.*	**that**	*That is John's car.*
Plural	**these**	*These glasses are mine.*	**those**	*Those cars are driving too fast.*

EXERCISE ❸   Write *this, that, these,* or *those* in the spaces provided.

EXAMPLE: What are _____*these*_____ marks on my shirt?

1. Look at _____ lights in the distance.

2. What is _____ strange round object in the sky?

3. Look out the window. _____ people are standing in the street.

4. Do you see _____ man outside? What is he doing?

5. Is _____ object a UFO?

6. I will use _____ binoculars to get a better look.

7. Right beside me there is a telescope. _____ telescope is also very useful.

8. What is happening in the world _____ days?

Articles

■ A, AN

A and *An* mean "one."

- Use *a* before nouns that begin with a consonant.   *a friend, a house*
  Exception: When *u* sounds like "you" put *a* before it.   *a union*
- Use *an* before nouns that begin with a vowel.   *an apple, an umbrella*
  Exception: Use *an* before words that begin with *silent h*.   *an honest man, an hour*

You cannot put *a* or *an* before a plural noun. Remember that *a* and *an* mean "one."

In English we put *a* or *an* before the names of professions. E.g., *I want to be **an** architect.*

CLASS EXERCISE

Put *a* or *an* before the following count nouns. Put X before plural nouns.

EXAMPLE: ___*A*___ doctor   ___*An*___ apple   ___*X*___ children

1. _____ hotel   **5.** _____ architect   **9.** _____ lonely people

2. _____ young women   **6.** _____ open envelope   **10.** _____ nice man

3. _____ hero   **7.** _____ fantastic dancer   **11.** _____ hour*

4. _____ small island   **8.** _____ umbrella   **12.** _____ hospital

* The word *hour* is pronounced *our* and the *h* is silent. In most words beginning with *h*, the *h* is pronounced.

EXERCISE ❹   Put *a*, *an*, or X (meaning *nothing*) in the spaces provided. Remember that you do not put *a* or *an* before a plural noun!

EXAMPLE: Koffman bikes are ___*X*___ great bikes.

1. Carl is _____ architect and I am _____ lawyer.

2. Carl often says that _____ apple every day keeps the doctor away.

3. Carl has _____ beautiful children. For their birthdays, they like to receive _____ money* and _____ gifts.

4. I live in _____ nice apartment. Carl doesn't live in _____ apartment. He owns _____ house.

5. I don't have _____ automobile, but I have _____ bicycle. Carl has _____ Mercedes.

6. Carl's daughter wants to be _____ engineer, and his son wants to be _____ veterinarian.

7. One day I want to own _____ ranch with _____ horses.

8. Carl's children have _____ homework* tonight.

* Some nouns have no plural form and cannot be counted, such as *money, music, information, homework, equipment,* and *baggage.* You cannot put *a* or *an* before these non-count nouns! There is a list of non-count nouns in your *Grammar Charts.* There is also an exercise about non-count nouns in Appendix 3 of this book, on page 105.

■ THE

Use *the* to indicate a specific noun (or specific nouns). *The* can be placed before singular or plural nouns.

<u>EXAMPLE:</u>   *I need to find **a** new shirt. **The** shirts in that store are expensive.*
                     general   specific

Do not put *the* before languages (*He studies Greek*), sports (*I play hockey*), city names, or most country names (*Karen lives in London but her sister moved to Spain*).

EXERCISE ❺   Put the noun in parentheses on the line provided. Add *the* if the noun refers to something specific. Do not use *the* when the statement is general.

1. (*babies*) _____ *Babies* _____ are cute. _____ *The babies* _____ in that advertisement are really cute.

2. (*diamonds*) _____ in that jewelry store are very expensive. _____ usually cost a lot of money.

3. (*money*) _____ is important for some people. Other people think that love is more important than _____. _____ on that table is mine.

4. (*milk*) _____ in that carton is goat's milk. Generally, _____ comes from cows and goats.

5. (candy) _____ usually contains a lot of sugar.

_____ in that box is sugar-free.

EXERCISE **6**   PART A: Put *the* or X (meaning *nothing*) in the spaces provided.

EXAMPLE: I like ___X___ art. I particulary like ___the___ art of Frida Kahlo.

1. _____ life is sometimes difficult. _____ life of Van Gogh was particularly rough.

2. Monica really wants to have _____ children one day. _____ children in the living room are mine.

3. _____ blue PT Cruiser in front of that store is very expensive. I prefer _____ Volkswagens.

4. I need _____ help. What is _____ answer to this question?

5. My brother loves _____ sports. He likes to play _____ tennis, _____ badminton and _____ hockey.

PART B (Review of *A, An* and *The*)

Put *a, an, the,* or X (meaning *nothing*) in the spaces provided.

EXAMPLE: Mark wants to read ___a___ book. The books are on ___the___ bookshelf.

6. I need _____ haircut. Where are _____ scissors that I put on that counter?

7. Mark's novels are about _____ life and _____ death. His most recent is about _____ life of Beethoven.

8. _____ boy sitting next to me is Claire's brother. I don't have _____ sister or _____ brother.

9. I can't speak _____ Greek, but I can speak _____ French and _____ Spanish.

10. Jeff likes _____ computers. _____ computer on that table belongs to him. I need _____ new computer.

ANOTHER / A LOT

Usually *an* is a separate word but when you put *an* before *other*, it becomes one word: *another*.

   I want ~~an other~~ piece of cake. (*another*)

A lot is always written as two separate words.

   Lennon wrote ~~alot~~ of songs. (*a lot*)

© Longman   Plurals and Articles   **61**

EXERCISE 7   The following sentences have an error with articles (*a, an, the*). Circle and correct the error, or add the missing article.

EXAMPLE: John Lennon was (a) interesting person.   *an*

1. Charlie Chaplin made a great movies.   _____

2. I have big picture of Charlie Chaplin on my wall.   _____

3. When I finish school, I want to be a actor.   _____

4. I don't have an other plan for my future.   _____

5. My sister wants to become marine biologist.   _____

6. When she was child, she loved dolphins.   _____

7. Dolphins live in ocean.   _____

8. There are alot of dolphins near Florida.   _____

Take Another Look

Answer the following questions. If you don't know an answer, then go back and review the appropriate section!

1. Can *a* or *an* be placed before a plural noun?   ❑ Yes   ❑ No

   Explain why: _____

2. Write *general* or *specific noun* on the line provided.

   Use *a / an* before _____ singular nouns.

   Use *the* before _____ nouns.

3. What is wrong with this sentence?   *She has many others subjects in school.*

   _____

4. Circle two expressions that are spelled correctly.

   an other   *another*   *a lot*   *alot*

5. Write *this*, *that*, *these* and *those* in the correct spaces.

   One object, near   _____   One object, far   _____

   Many objects, near   _____   Many objects, far   _____

CLASS EXERCISE (REVIEW)

PART A: If the sentence is correct, write *C* in the space provided. If the sentence has a plural-form error, correct it in the space provided.

EXAMPLE: I enjoy simples stories.   *simple stories*

1. Canadian musicians are very populars.   _____

2. There are many differents songs on Shania's CD.   _____

3. Millions of persons buy Celine's music.   _____

4. There are four men in the Ontario band, Sum 41.   _____

5. Childrens under age 12 cannot attend the show.   _____

6. Many teenager are dancing in the mosh pit.   _____

7. There are many theorys about the success
   of Canadian artists.   _____

PART B: Circle the letter of the best answer.

8. Look outside! ... cars just had an accident!
   a) This   **b)** That   **c)** Those   **d)** There

9. My brother lives in ... apartment with his friends.
   a) a   **b)** an   **c)** the   **d)** (nothing)

10. My brother, Danny, is ... big music fan.
    a) a   **b)** an   **c)** the   **d)** (nothing)

11. Danny has ... of CDs. He has ... ninety CDs in his bedroom.
    a) a lot / a   **b)** alot / a   **c)** a lot / (nothing)   **d)** alot / (nothing)

12. We need to meet at ... time. I have ... appointment at 7:30.
    a) another / an   **b)** an other / an   **c)** another / the   **d)** an other / the

13. We are in an auditorium. ... auditorium has room for 5000 spectators.
    a) This   **b)** It   **c)** These   **d)** There

14. There is ... amazing performer at the concert.
    a) a   **b)** an   **c)** the   **d)** (nothing)

15. Yukio lives in ... Japan. She is ... performance artist.
    a) the / a   **b)** the / an   **c)** (nothing) / an   **d)** (nothing) / a

8 Future Tenses

"Will" and "(Be) Going To"

Both *will* and *(be) going to* indicate a future action.

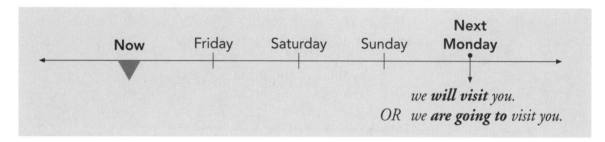

Key words: soon, later, tomorrow, the day after tomorrow, next week, next month, one day, in five years…

Will

AFFIRMATIVE		QUESTION FORM MOVE *WILL* BEFORE THE SUBJECT			NEGATIVE FORM ADD *NOT*	
I She He It You We They	will eat.	Will	I she he it you we they	eat?	I She He It You We They	will not eat. (won't)

(Be) going to

AFFIRMATIVE			QUESTION FORM MOVE *BE* BEFORE THE SUBJECT			NEGATIVE FORM ADD *NOT*		
I	am		Am	I		I	am	
She	is		Is	she		She	is	
He	is		Is	he		He	is	
It	is	going to eat.	Is	it	going to eat?	It	is	not going to eat.
We	are		Are	we		We	are	
You	are		Are	you		You	are	
They	are		Are	they		They	are	

EXERCISE 1 Fill in the blanks with the future tenses. Use both *will* and *be going to*.

EXAMPLE: Karl (visit) _____*is going to visit*_____ his mother next Friday. OR

Karl (visit) _____*will visit*_____ his mother next Friday.

1. Tam (be) _____ 17 years old tomorrow. OR

   Tam (be) _____ 17 years old tomorrow.

2. What (you, do) _____ during your next vacation? OR

   What (you, do) _____ during your next vacation?

3. It (snow, not) _____ next weekend. OR

   It (snow, not) _____ next weekend.

■ *WILL VS. (BE) GOING TO*

When you make a prediction about the future or discuss a future event, you can use *will* or *be going to*.

>   It **is going to rain** tomorrow.   It **will rain** tomorrow.

Some exceptions:

- Use *going to* if something is definitely going to happen.
  *Tomorrow, the town **is going to turn off** the water supply.*   (This is a definite plan.)

- Use *will* to express a spontaneous decision or to indicate that you are volunteering to do something. You can contract the pronoun and will: *I'll, she'll,* etc.
  *The doorbell is ringing. **I'll answer** it.*   (This is a spontaneous decision.)
  *Who will bring the coffee next week? **I'll bring** it.*   (This is a voluntary action.)

EXERCISE 2 Fill in the blanks with the future tense of the verb. Use either *will, be going to*, or indicate that both future tenses are possible.

EXAMPLE: One day I (go) _____*will go OR am going to go*_____ to university.

Jerry and I (see) _____*are going to see*_____ a movie at 7 PM.

She is choking! I (save) _____*will save*_____ her!

1. The phone is ringing. I (get) _____ it.

2. Someone needs to buy more bread. Vera said that she (go) _____ to the bakery.

3. One day I (be) _____ rich.

4. The kettle is boiling. I (turn) _____ it off.

5. The electric company called. They (turn) _____ off our power tonight.

6. Next year I (stay) _____ in college.

7. When I graduate, I (find) _____ a good job.

8. The boss (fire) _____ Julie tomorrow. He has no choice.

Remember: Most of the time, you can use both *will* and *be going to*.

EXERCISE ❸ **PART A:** Read the sentences about the space station. Make the verb negative.

<u>EXAMPLE:</u>   Those scientists *will find* alien life. _____ *won't find* _____

1. The space station *will be* ready soon.   _____

2. Yuri *will go* into space next year.   _____

3. Yuri *is going to stay* in the space station.   _____

4. The space station *will orbit* the earth.   _____

5. Some astronauts *are going to spend*
a year there.   _____

PART B: Make yes/no questions. Change the subject to a subject pronoun.

<u>EXAMPLE:</u>   Mr. Kelsey *will help* me. _____ *Will he help me?* _____

6. The program *is going to cost* a lot.

_____

7. Some people *will visit* the site.

_____

8. Mark and Jody *are going to apply* for the job.

_____

9. Two scientists *will grow* food there.

_____

10. Yuri *will work* hard.

_____

Short Answers

You can answer questions with short answers. Simply repeat the subject and the auxiliary. It is not necessary to repeat the verb.

Will you help me? → *Yes, I will.*   OR → *No, I won't.*
Are you happy? → *Yes, I am.*   OR → *No, I am not.* (or *I'm not*)

EXERCISE 4   Answer the following questions with a "yes" and a "no" short answer.

<u>EXAMPLE:</u>   Will you come home soon?

Yes, I _____ *will* .   No, I _____ *won't* .

1. Are you working right now?

Yes, I _____   No, I _____

2. Is Ted going to pay you tomorrow?

Yes, he _____   No, he _____

3. Did Jason finish his report last night?

Yes, he _____   No, he _____

4. Will you pass me that hammer?

Yes, I _____   No, I _____

5. Do you want to buy jewelry?

Yes, I _____   No, I _____

6. Does Ben have a computer?

Yes, he _____   No, he _____

7. Are they going to eat lunch soon?

Yes, they _____   No, they _____

8. Will mom help Tim finish his project?

Yes, she _____   No, she _____

9. Did you go to the butcher shop yesterday?

Yes, we _____   No, we _____

10. Will you give me some chocolate?

Yes, I _____   No, I _____

NEVER WRITE "GONNA"

English-speaking people often say "gonna" to mean "going to." However, it is unacceptable to write "gonna."

going to
I'm go~~nna~~ call you.

EXERCISE ⑤ Identify and correct the errors. If the sentence has no error, write "C" in the space provided.

EXAMPLE: What are you (gonna) do later?   *going to*

1. Mike Myers is gonna make more *Austin Powers* movies.   _____

2. Why Mike is going to move to London?   _____

3. Jeff is gonna be an actor one day.   _____

4. When will you drive me to the cinema?   _____

5. Do we will probably be late?   _____

6. Will I come to a restaurant with you? No, I am not.   _____

7. Mike probably won't work on television again.   _____

8. When is the movie is going to begin?   _____

9. When are you gonna pay for the tickets?   _____

10. What movie is Mike going to make next year?   _____

Present, Past, and Future Tense Review

EXERCISE ⑥ Add the verb in parentheses to each group of sentences. Write the verb in the correct tense.

EXAMPLE: **(study)**

Omar _____*is going to study*_____ OR _____*will study*_____ next week.

Omar _____*is studying*_____ right now.

Omar _____*studied*_____ yesterday.

Omar _____*studies*_____ every Saturday.

1. **(write)**

   Sarah _____ OR _____ a song next week.

   Sarah _____ a song now.

   Sarah _____ a song yesterday.

   Sarah _____ new songs every week.

2. **(be, not)**

   They _____ OR _____ angry next week.

   They _____ angry now.

   They _____ angry yesterday.

3. (do, not)

Mr. Roy _____ OR _____ his work next week.

Mr. Roy _____ his work now.

Mr. Roy _____ his work yesterday.

Mr. Roy often _____ his work.

4. (work — *Question forms*)

Where _____ those women usually _____?

Where _____ those women _____ last year?

Where _____ those women _____ next year? OR

Where _____ those women _____ next year?

Take Another Look

Answer the following questions. If you don't know an answer, then go back and review the appropriate section.

1. Circle the key words which indicate a future time.

    tomorrow   last week   next week   in three weeks   three weeks ago

2. What is the negative form of **will**? _____

3. Is "gonna" a proper word?   ❏ Yes   ❏ No

4. What are the question and negative forms of the following sentences?

    a) She will help us.

        Yes/No question form   _____

        Negative form   _____

    b) We are going to go.

        Yes/No question form   _____

        Negative form   _____

    c) He is going to laugh.

        Yes/No question form   _____

        Negative form   _____

CLASS EXERCISE (REVIEW)

PART A: Circle the letter of the correct answer.

1. What (she, wear) ... to the party next week?

    a) will she wears   **b)** are she going to wear

    c) will she wear   **d)** she will wear

2. I (drive, not) … tomorrow because I don't have my driver's license.
   a) won't to drive
   b) am not going to drive
   c) am not gonna drive
   d) do not drive

3. You (be, not) … ready for next Monday's test if you watch TV all weekend.
   a) won't are
   b) will not to be
   c) won't is
   d) won't be

4. In the future, my brother (move) … to Miami.
   a) will move
   b) is gonna move
   c) will moves
   d) move

5. Martin (come) … to the film with us next Friday.
   a) will comes
   b) will come
   c) will came
   d) are going to come

PART B: Identify and correct the future tense errors. There are five errors in spelling, tense form, or question forms.

EXAMPLE: Ms. Rather (willn't visit) you next Thursday.
won't

Francis *is gone to go* to military school next year. He probably *won't like it* because

the school is very strict. His father *is gonna ask* Francis to stay in the school. Francis and

his friend, Andrew, *is going to take* the bus to their new school. Mr. Andrews *wo'nt drive*

the boys to their school. Why *is Francis is going to go* to such a strict school?

Wrap Up

■ TALK ABOUT FUTURE PREDICTIONS

Work with a team of students and come up with five predictions about the future.
What will the world be like one hundred years from now? Think about the following areas:

- transport
- fashion
- communication
- family life
- politics
- science

Write down one sentence for each area. Your team should work together to compose the sentences.

9 Modals

Modal auxiliaries are a special class of words. These words indicate things such as ability (*can*) and obligation (*must*). Modals differ from other verbs in the following way:

- Modals have no 3rd person singular form.
  Compare: *Vince **helps** people.*   *Vince **can help** you.*

FUNCTION	MODAL	EXAMPLE	NEGATIVE FORM
Ability Past ability	can could	She **can** speak English. She **could** speak Greek when she was young.	cannot (can't) could not (couldn't)
Polite requests	may would could can	**May** I help you? **Would** you like some coffee? **Could** you pass the butter? **Can** I have some help?	
Possibility	could might may	Daniel **could** help you. Mary **might** do the job. Ann **may** help them.	could not (couldn't) might not may not
Advice	should	Alan **should** see a lawyer.	should not (shouldn't)
Obligation Past obligation	must have to* had to	Jason **must** work now. She **has to** go to the hospital. Yesterday she **had to** work late.	must not does not have to did not have to
Conditional	will would	If I have time, I **will** help you. (It is possible.) If I had time, I **would** help her. (It is not likely)	will not (won't) would not (wouldn't)

* Although "have to" is not a modal auxiliary, it is included on this list because it functions like a modal, and it has the same meaning as *must*.

CLASS EXERCISE

Answer the following questions.

1. Which sentence is most polite?
   a) Do I have to help you?
   b) May I help you?
   c) Should I help you?

2. Which two sentences have the same meaning?
   a) We may go to a movie later.
   b) We can go to a movie later.
   c) We might go to a movie later.

3. Who has no choice?
   a) Dr. Suyu must take a vacation.
   b) Dr. Benoit should take a vacation.
   c) Dr. Roy can take a vacation.

4. Which two sentences have the same meaning?
   a) Jason should study tonight.
   b) Alexia must study tonight.
   c) Zelda has to study tonight.

EXERCISE 1 Look at the following sentences. Then answer the questions that follow.

- *Maruka* **can speak** *five languages, but she* **can't write** *in those languages.*
- **Can you speak** *several languages? I* **cannot speak** *Greek or Spanish.*

1. **Can** indicates: (choose one)   **a)** ability   **b)** obligation   **c)** advice.

2. When the subject is third-person singular, do you add "s" to **can**?   ❑ Yes   ❑ No

   Do you add "s" to the verb that follows **can**?   ❑ Yes   ❑ No

3. In question forms, does **can** go before or after the subject? _____

4. What are the two negative forms of **can**? _____   _____

Can — Could

- Can indicates a present ability.   *I* **can ski**.
- Could indicates a past ability.   *When Mr. Mukerjee was younger,*
                                                       he **could ski***, but now he can't.*

   Could also means that something is possible.   *I* **could help** *you carry those bags.*

EXERCISE 2 Write a modal in the space provided. The function of the modal is stated.

   EXAMPLE: When Kelly was young, she (**past ability** / skate) _____*could skate*_____ ,
              but now she can't.

1. Alex (**present ability** / speak) _____ French and Italian.

2. Patrick (**past ability** / swim) _____ for miles, but now he can't.

3. My cat (**past ability** / chase) _____ mice, but now my cat

   (**present ability** / not, run) _____ quickly anymore.

4. When Tom was a child, he (**past ability** / not, read) _____
   until he was nine years old.

5. Five years ago I (**past ability** / not, speak) _____ Spanish,

   but now I (**present ability** / speak) _____ it quite well.

Polite Requests

EXERCISE 3 Read the following dialogue and circle the word that is most appropriate.

1. Waiter: (*May / Would / Should*) I help you?

2. Jason: Yes. I (*would / may / can*) like some wine.

(*May / Would*) I please see the wine list?

Waiter: Certainly.

3. Jason: (*Could / Would*) I taste the Bocciano wine?

4. Waiter: No. You can only taste the wine after you order it.

(*Could / May / Would*) you like a bottle of Bocciano wine?

5. Jason: No thanks. (*May / Can*) you bring me a glass of water?

6. Waiter: Certainly. (*Could / Would*) I offer you something to eat?

7. Jason: Yes. I (*may / would / could*) like a piece of toast, please.

8. Waiter: Certainly. (*Would / Could / May*) you like anything else?

9. Jason: No. (*Could / May / Should*) you please bring me my toast and water?

Obligation vs. Advice

a) Use "should" when you want to give advice: *You **should** stop smoking.*

b) Use "must" or "have to" to express necessity: *I **have to** work late tonight.*
*I **must** leave.*

EXERCISE 4   In the spaces provided, insert the correct modal auxiliary +verb.

<u>EXAMPLE:</u>   You (*advice*, leave) _____ *should leave* _____ now.

He (*necessity*, leave) _____ *has to leave OR must leave* _____ now.

1. Yuri (*necessity*, walk) _____ to the stadium
every day.

2. The wind is cold. You (*advice*, wear) _____ a hat.

3. Yuri (*necessity*, play) _____ really well next
week.

4. The baseball players (*advice*, accept) _____
the contract. The terms are very good for them.

5. The team (*necessity*, win) _____ if it wants to
make the playoffs.

6. The coach (*advice*, encourage) _____ the
players. They look dejected.

Negative Forms

Examine the negative forms of the following modals.

Statement	Negative	Neg. contraction
He should work harder.	*He **should not** work harder.*	*(shouldn't)*
He can stay home.	*He **cannot stay** home.*	*(can't)*

Have to requires an auxiliary (*do* or *does*) in the negative and question forms.

Brian has to do it.	*Brian **does not have to** do it.*	*(doesn't have to)*

EXERCISE 5 **PART A:** Write the modals in their contracted, negative forms.

EXAMPLE: I can _____ *can't* _____

1. He *would* _____

2. She *has to* _____

3. She *should* _____

4. We *have to* _____

5. They *could* _____

6. We *can* _____

PART B: Make the italicized verbs in the following sentences negative.

EXAMPLE: Moira *should visit* us. _____ *should not visit (OR shouldn't)* _____

7. Yuri *can come* with me. _____

8. She *has to go* home now. _____

9. You *should buy* a new uniform. _____

10. We *have to work* late. _____

Question Forms

Modals are auxiliaries. To form a question, move the modal before the subject.

Statement	Question form
I (can) swim.	(**Can**) you swim?
She should leave.	***Should** she leave?*

Have to is a regular verb. You must add an auxiliary (*do, does, did*) to the question form.

Henry has to work late.	***Does** he **have to** work late?*

EXERCISE 6 Write questions. Change the subject to a subject pronoun. The exact answer is in bold.

EXAMPLE: Neil should meet us **at 10 PM**. _____ *When should he meet us?* _____

1. Mr. Sen could meet us **after the storm**.

_____

2. Kelly should wear **a warm coat** during the storm.

_____

3. Marnie can hide **in the basement**.

_____

4. Those tourists could stay in **a storm shelter**.

_____

5. Sarah has to buy **more groceries** later.

_____

6. We should find **a flashlight**.

_____

7. Kelly would like to stay **in our house**.

_____

8. They have to leave their home **because a hurricane is coming**.

_____

EXERCISE 7 There is one error in each of the following sentences. Identify the error and then write the correct word in the space provided.

EXAMPLE: Eric _must ~~to~~ leave_ now.   _____ _must leave_ _____

1. Carlos _should helps_ me study.   _____

2. When I was a child, I _can't understand_ Spanish, but now I can.   _____

3. I _can to speak_ very well when I travel to Mexico.   _____

4. When _Carlos can teach_ me Italian?   _____

5. _May you practice_ with me sometimes?   _____

6. I know that you _don't can do_ it now because you are busy.   _____

7. _Do I could offer_ you some coffee?   _____

8. I suppose that you _must to leave_ soon.   _____

9. We *should to visit* each other more often. _____

10. Carlos looks ill. I think that he *shoulds visit* a doctor. _____

Take Another Look

Answer the following questions. If you don't know an answer, then go back and review the appropriate section!

1. What is the present-tense, third-person singular form of **have to**? _____

2. With all other modals, is there a third-person singular form? ❑ Yes ❑ No

3. What are the question and negative forms of the following sentences?

   a) We should leave.

   Yes/No question form _____

   Negative form _____

   b) He can read.

   Yes/No question form _____

   Negative form _____

   c) They could help.

   Yes/No question form _____

   Negative form _____

   d) She has to study.

   Yes/No question form _____

   Negative form _____

   e) They have to go.

   Yes/No question form _____

   Negative form _____

CLASS EXERCISE (REVIEW)

PART A: Each of the following sentences contains an error, shown in italics. Write the correct word(s) in the space provided.

EXAMPLE: *Do you can go?* _____ *Can you go?* _____

1. The doctor *should examines* her soon. _____

2. *Why Donald has to* come with us? _____

3. Yukio *cans speak* Japanese very well. _____

4. *Do you could give* me more coffee please? _____

5. *She would likes* another cup of coffee please. _____

PART B: Circle the letter of the best answer.

6. Where … for lunch today?
   a) we should go
   b) do we should go
   c) should we go

7. Carolyn … because she has another appointment.
   a) must leaves
   b) has to leave
   c) have to leave

8. When I was a teenager, I … four servings of food. Now I can only eat one serving.
   a) could eat
   b) could ate
   c) can ate

9. … the television?
   a) Can she repairs
   b) Can she can repair
   c) Can she repair

10. Why … the project by himself?
    a) should Robert do
    b) Robert should do
    c) should Robert does

Wrap Up

■ TALK ABOUT ADVICE LETTERS

Read the following letters. With a partner, or in teams of three, discuss what the letter writer should do. Then write down your advice. Explain what the letter writers should do and why.

1. My parents got divorced. Now my father expects me to tell him about my mother's activities. He asks me who she dates, and he wants to know if men come to the house. Should I tell my father about my mother's activities?

   Alex

2. I am 16 years old and I am very lonely. I have a hard time meeting people. I recently met a nice guy on the Internet. He is nineteen and he lives in another city. He wants to send me a bus ticket to visit him. Should I go?

   Paula

3. I broke up with a guy six months ago. Now he is dating my best friend. I regret breaking up with him. I want us to get back together. Should I try to get him back?

   Lynda

10 Comparisons

Adjectives

Adjectives give information about nouns.

- Adjectives generally appear before the nouns that they modify (or after the verb *be*).
- Adjectives are never plural.

<u>EXAMPLE:</u> Giraffes are *tall, intelligent, and beautiful* **animals**.

Adjectives before the noun (no plural form!)

EXERCISE 1 In each sentence, the final noun and adjective(s) are in bold. Underline the final noun. Then correct the error in adjective form or word order.

<u>EXAMPLE:</u> Lucy has <u>**eyes**</u> **blues**. _____*blue eyes*_____

1. I am a **girl 17 years old**. _____

2. My family often visits **others countries**. _____

3. We stayed in Mexico for **two years and a half**. _____

4. Our hotel room had no **paper toilet**. _____

5. In Mexico we met two **very nices people**. _____

6. Ricardo is a **person very active**. _____

7. He likes to be with **others people**. _____

8. Now we are back in **ours house**. _____

9. My father doesn't like us to wear **brand names shoes**. _____

10. We also can't watch **musics videos**. _____

Comparatives and Superlatives

■ ONE-SYLLABLE ADJECTIVES / ADJECTIVES ENDING IN Y

SPELLING OF COMPARATIVE AND SUPERLATIVE FORMS	ADJECTIVE	COMPARATIVE	SUPERLATIVE
• For one-syllable adjectives, add **er** or **est**.	tall	tall**er** than	the tall**est**
• If the adjective finishes in one vowel followed by one consonant, you should double the last letter.	thin	thi**nner** than	the thi**nnest**
• If the adjective ends in consonant-y, change the **y** to **i** and add **er** or **est**.	happy	happ**ier** than	the happ**iest**
• If the adjective ends in an **e**, just add **r** or **st**.	cute	cute**r** than	the cute**st**

■ LONG ADJECTIVES

To compare adjectives of two or more syllables, use the words *more … than*.
For the superlative form, add *the most …* before the adjective.

ADJECTIVE	COMPARATIVE	SUPERLATIVE
modern	more modern than	the most modern
interesting	more interesting than	the most interesting

EXERCISE 2   Write the following adjectives in their comparative and superlative forms.

Comparative Form   Superlative Form

EXAMPLE: short _____*shorter than*_____   _____*the shortest*_____

1. nice _____   _____

2. unusual _____   _____

3. soft _____   _____

4. lazy _____   _____

5. dynamic _____   _____

6. easy _____   _____

7. big _____   _____

8. funny _____   _____

9. exciting _____   _____

10. reasonable _____   _____

■ IRREGULAR ADJECTIVES

The following adjectives have an irregular comparative and superlative form.

ADJECTIVE	COMPARATIVE	SUPERLATIVE
good	*better than*	*the best*
bad	*worse than*	*the worst*

EXERCISE 3 Complete the sentences with the appropriate comparative or superlative form. Remember to add "than" after the comparative form or "the" before the superlative form.

1. In the 1980s, Wayne Gretzky was (good) _____ hockey player in Canada.

2. Tiger Woods' golf clubs are (expensive) _____ mine are.

3. Tiger Woods uses (expensive) _____ golf equipment in the world.

4. I use (cheap) _____ golf equipment in the world.

5. Tiger Woods is (young) _____ other pro golfers.

6. Eli Williams is (bad) _____ Tiger Williams at golf.

7. I am (bad) _____ athlete in my neighborhood.

8. I think that Mohammed Ali was (great) _____ boxer in history.

9. I am tired, but Eli is (tired) _____ I am.

10. Who is (happy) _____ person that you know?

Equality: "as ... as" / "the same as"

Both *as....as* and *the same as* express equality.

> *Sharon is **as smart as** Doug.*
> *My car is **the same as** yours.*

Sometimes one object is not *as good as* another.

> *High heels are **not as comfortable as** running shoes.*

EXERCISE 4   Write the correct form of the adjectives. You may need to use the comparative or superlative forms, or you may need to use *as ... as*. There are key words in each sentence to help you.

- If you see *as*, use *as ... as*.   *My dog is (obedient)* __*as obedient*__ **as** *your dog.*
- If you see *than*, use the comparative form.   *My dog is* __*lazier*__ **than** *your dog.*
- If you see *the*, use the superlative form.   *Tia's house is* **the** *(big)* __*biggest*__ *house on our street.*

1. I don't like my new apartment. It is (small) _____ than my old one. It is also (cold) _____ than my old one. Basically, my new apartment is not (good) _____ as my old apartment.

2. Michael plays baseball, but he is not (good) _____ as Eduardo. Eduardo is the (good) _____ player on our team.

3. My grandmother is usually (active) _____ than I am. In the past, my grandmother could run around the park, but she had a heart attack last summer. Now she is not (healthy) _____ as she was in the past.

4. My father thinks that today's music is (bad) _____ than music in the past. He says that the Beatles were the (great) _____ band in history, and he thinks that no group is (interesting) _____ as the Beatles. He often says that today's musicians are (lazy) _____ than past musicians. I disagree with him. I think that today's musicians are (good) _____ as past musicians. In fact, some of today's groups are (good) _____ than the Beatles!

EXERCISE 5   There is one error in each of the following sentences. Circle and correct each error.

EXAMPLE: I work as hard (than) Philippe does.
                               as

1. Jim Carrey is more funnier than Adam Sandler.

2. That comedian is in same movie as Adam Sandler.

3. Kramer is a worst singer than Adam is.

4. My brother thinks that Adam's movie is more better than Jim's movie.

5. Robin Williams is older then Jim Carrey.

6. Many of best comedians were born in Canada.

7. Robin is crazyer than Jim.

8. Robert is the better actor in the world.

9. Jim is more active that Adam.

10. Adam does not earn the same salary than Jim.

THAN, THEN, THAT

Here are the basic differences between *than*, *then*, and *that*.

Than: This is used in sentences in which two things are compared.
*I am older **than** you are. You have more food **than** I do.*

Then: This word means "next" or "after that."
*We sold the company and **then** we moved to Florida.*

That: *That* is used in several different ways. First, it can be used when you give more information about a subject.
*Can you return the book **that** I gave you?*

That also means the same thing as "this," except *that* implies distance.
*Bruce was hired by **that** company.*

EXERCISE 6 Identify the errors in the usage of *then*, *than*, or *that*. If an incorrect term is used, circle it and write the correct term above it. There are seven errors, not including the example.

that

1. I really love music. I especially love the music (than) John Lennon wrote. When I was

   a child, my father played a tape of John Lennon's music. I thought *than* the singer

   sounded funny. *Than*, when I got older, I learned to appreciate Lennon's music.

2. It is a pity *than* John Lennon died. He made his last record and *then* a crazy man shot

   him. Lennon made music *than* everybody liked. He wrote more songs *then* most

   other songwriters. I think *than* he was the best musician in the twentieth century.

   He was definitely a better songwriter *then* Madonna.

Take Another Look

Ask yourself the following questions. If you don't know an answer, go back and check the appropriate section.

1. What ending do you add to short (one-syllable) adjectives in the comparative form? _____

2. What ending do you add to short adjectives in the superlative form? _____

3. What two forms express that two items have equal value?

   _____   _____

4. What are the comparative and superlative forms of the following adjectives?

	Comparative form	Superlative form
a) good	_____	_____
b) bad	_____	_____
c) nice	_____	_____
d) happy	_____	_____
e) modern	_____	_____

CLASS EXERCISE (REVIEW)

PART A: Write the comparative or superlative forms of the following adjectives. Do not use "as ... as."

EXAMPLE: My sister is (young) _____*younger than*_____ I am.

1. This restaurant is (expensive) _____ that one.

2. Soup is (cheap) _____ item on the menu.

3. The Mexican hot sauce is (spicy) _____ the white sauce.

4. The sugar pie is (bad) _____ the apple pie.

5. In my opinion, the chocolate fudge cake is (good) _____ the carrot cake.

6. This coffee is disgusting. It is (bad) _____ coffee that I have ever tasted!

(continued →)

PART B: There is one error in each of the following sentences. Correct each error.

EXAMPLE:

$\overset{as}{}$

The cake is as tasty ~~than~~ the pie.

7. I ate at Moe's Diner and you ate at Jim's Deli. I didn't eat in the same restaurant than you.

8. The tea is colder that the coffee.

9. Vinnie is a baker. He thinks that his cake is the better cake in the world.

10. The waiter is very slow. We would like more better service.

Wrap Up

■ COMPARE

Compare yourself to your family members or friends. Write sentences using comparative and superlative forms. Use the following adjectives in your sentences.

good in English	organized	lazy
messy	rich	bad in sports
cute	crazy	hard working

EXAMPLE: My father is better in English than I am.
My mother is the most organized in my family.

Write your sentences on a separate piece of paper.

11 Word Choice

Infinitives ("to go, to come, to visit...")

Generally, when a verb is followed by another verb, use the infinitive (*to + base form*) of the second verb. If the verb is followed by a noun, no "to" is necessary.

We really need **to talk**.   We need more money.

Infinitive form of verb   Noun

EXERCISE ① Combine the words in parentheses. Use the correct tense of the verb!

EXAMPLE: We sometimes (try / speak / German) _____ *try to speak German* _____ .

1. On birthdays, Kim (prefer / receive / clothing) _____ .

2. Today I (need / money / buy) _____ a gift for Kim.

3. Kim (like / expensive clothing) _____ .

4. Yesterday Kim (try / cook) _____ dinner but

   we (refuse / let) _____ her cook.

5. When I was a child, my mother always (force / me / play) _____

   _____ outside.

6. Now I (like / not / stay) _____ indoors.

7. Every weekend Kim (play / chess) _____ with
   her friend.

8. Generally Kim (like / not / watch / TV) _____ .

BE CAREFUL

Never put *for* and *to* together! Generally use the infinitive form of the second verb!

to have

She is ready ~~for to have~~ her massage.

Never put *s* or *ed* on infinitives!

to visit

Mary tried ~~to visited~~ us yesterday.

EXERCISE 2 Each sentence has one infinitive mistake. Correct the error.

EXAMPLE:

to

The doctor likes ↑ work with sleep-deprived patients.

1. Marie wants to meet the doctor for to explain her problem.

2. According to the doctor, Marie needs get more sleep.

3. People should get at least seven hours of sleep each night for to have good health.

4. Marie likes to studies until 1 AM every night.

5. She wants to have good marks for to enter medical school.

6. She hopes to received the highest marks in her class.

7. She thinks that she must work hard for to have success.

8. Now she understands that she doesn't need have the best marks.

9. Maybe you should ask Marie for prepare for her exams.

10. Students should balance school and work if they want succeed.

Commonly Confused Words

TO, TOO, TWO

- *Too* means *excessive* or *also*.   *I have **too** much homework **too**.*
- *Two* is the number 2.   *We meet every **two** weeks.*
- *To* is a preposition.   *I want **to** go **to** Europe.*

WHERE VS. WERE

- *Where* is a question word to ask about a place.   ***Where** are my shoes?*
- *Were* is the past form of the verb *be*.   *We **were** late yesterday.*

LIFE, LIVE, LEAVE

- *Life* is a noun. The plural form is *lives*.   *I have a good **life**.*
- *Live* is a verb.   *I want to **live** with you.*
- *Leave* means "to go away from."   *He is rude. Ask him to **leave**.*

EXERCISE ③ Before each set of sentences, there are some words in parentheses. Put those words in the spaces provided.

EXAMPLE: (two, to, too) Lee went _____*to*_____ Las Vegas with _____*two*_____ friends.

(life, live, leave)

1. My _____ is very good now. I want to _____ for eighty years.

2. Dan wants to _____ in the country. He doesn't like city _____. He would like to _____ the city and move to the country as soon as possible.

3. My great grandfather had a very interesting _____.

(to, two, too)

4. The boys are _____ tired to watch TV. They should go _____ bed now.

5. I am very tired _____. I studied for _____ hours tonight.

6. Please wake me up at _____ o'clock in the morning. Everyday I go _____ work at that time.

(where, were)

7. _____ _____ you born?

8. When _____ you born?

9. Do you know _____ my pen is?

REALLY VS. VERY

Both *really* and *very* can mean "extremely."

Very: Do not put *very* before verbs. Put *very* before adjectives.
*That food is **very** good.*   *Jason is **very** tall.*   *I am **very** happy.*

Really: You can put *really* before adjectives and verbs.
*I **really** like that movie.*   *She is **really** nice.*
                really
I ~~very~~ like that movie.

EXERCISE ④ Correct the word-choice error or spelling error in the following sentences. If there is no error, write C beside the sentence.

1. I very like humorous films.   _____

2. Some movies are to long and to boring.   _____

3. Last night I very wanted to watch a Jim Carrey movie. _____

4. Jim Carrey is a very funny guy. _____

5. On TV, there was a movie about Andy Kaufman's live. _____

6. I very appreciate Jim Carrey's comedy style. _____

7. Did you know that Jim Carrey used to leave
in Ontario, Canada? _____

8. Many people's lifes are very difficult. _____

9. Jim didn't have an easy live. _____

10. There where many people who influenced Jim. _____

HIS VS. IS

- *Is* is a form of the verb *be*.   *Where **is** my coat?*
- *His* is a possessive adjective.   *John took **his** kids to the mall.*

AS VS. HAS

- *Has* is the third-person singular form of the verb *have*.   *Spain **has** many beaches.*
- *As* is used to compare things of equal value.   *This is **as** good **as** it gets!*

EXERCISE 5   Circle the letter of the best answer.

1. What kind of … do you want to have?

   a) live   **b)** life   **c)** lived

2. Raymond often discusses … problems during lunch. He … very unhappy these days.

   a) his / is   **b)** is / his   **c)** is / is

3. I tried … learn how to speak Greek but it was … difficult for me. I cannot speak Greek.

   a) (nothing) / too   **b)** to / too   **c)** too / too   **d)** too / to

4. Why … the boys so late yesterday? And … are the boys now?

   a) where / where   **b)** was / where   **c)** were / were   **d)** were / where

5. David … likes to repair his own car. He … an expensive, antique Ford.

   a) really / has   **b)** very / as   **c)** really / as   **d)** very / has

6. Elian and Gloria have … cars, but they want … sell one car.

   a) to / to   **b)** two / too   **c)** two / to   **d)** two / (nothing)

7. Mr. Bergen … two children. He is teaching … son, David, how to drive a car.

   a) as / is   **b)** has / is   **c)** as / his   **d)** has / his

8. ... were you yesterday? I think you party ... much.

a) Where / to   **b)** Were / too   **c)** Where / too   **d)** Were / to

---

SOME AND ANY

- Affirmative sentences — Use *some*.   *There is **something** in my soup.*
- Negative sentences — Use *any*.*   *No. There isn't **anything** in your soup.*
- Questions — Use *some* or *any*.   *Do you want **some** soup? Do you want **any** bread?*

* Note: *Any* also means "it doesn't matter which."   *Eat any fruit that you want.*

This rule also applies to *something, somewhere, someone,* and *anything, anywhere, anyone.*

EXERCISE ⑥

1. Put *some* or *any* in the spaces.

Anne: Would you like _____ tea?

Joe: Yes, I'd love _____ tea, but I don't want

_____ cream or sugar.

Anne: I need _____ money to pay for a new car. Could you give me

_____ money?

Joe: No, you won't get _____ money from me.

2. Put *someone* or *anyone* in the spaces.

Joe: Is there a grocery store near here?

Anne: I don't know. You'll have to ask _____ else.

Joe: But you don't understand. I don't know _____ in this town!

3. Put *something* or *anything* in the spaces.

Joe: Do you want _____ expensive for your birthday?

Anne: No. Please don't spend money. I don't want _____ .

Joe: You are acting silly. Of course I will buy you _____ .

NO VS. ANY

The following sentences have the same negative meaning. To give *any* a negative meaning, you must add the word "not" to the sentence. *No* has a negative meaning.

    *I **don't** have **any** time.*   *I have **no** time.*
    *I **don't** want **anything** to eat.*   *I want **nothing** to eat.*

If you write *I want anything to eat,* it means: "it doesn't matter which thing."

EXERCISE 7 Change the sentences and write *any* instead of *no*. You will have to add negative verb forms. Remember that both sentences have the same meaning.

EXAMPLE: I want no coffee.   *I don't want any coffee.*

1. I got no gifts for my birthday.   _____

2. We know nobody.   _____

3. There are no girls in our class.   _____

4. There is no money in the jar.   _____

5. Ellen has no friends.   _____

6. We need no help.   _____

7. I want nothing for my birthday.   _____

WATCH, LOOK, AND LISTEN

Watch

We *watch* something that is moving. For example, we *watch* a movie. We *watch* people who pass by.

> *Did you* **watch** *TV last night?*

Look at

We *look at* something that is immobile. For example, we *look at* a picture. We *look at* a house. Follow *look* with the preposition *at*.

> **Look at** *me!* **Look at** *this picture!*

Look for

We *look for* (or *search for*) an object that is lost. For example, if we lose our keys, we *look for* them.

> *Help me* **look for** *my keys. I can't find them.*

Listen to

We *listen to* something that makes noise. Although in French it is correct to say "We listen to TV," in English we watch TV. We *listen to* the radio. Always follow *listen* with *to*.

> *He rarely* **listens to** *music.*

EXERCISE 8 Most of the following sentences contain a word-choice error. In some sentences, the correct term is used but it is followed by the incorrect preposition. Correct the error in each sentence. If the sentence is correct, write *C* in the space provided.

Remember: you *watch TV* and you *listen to music*.

EXAMPLE: *to*

I am listening ↑ a new CD.

1. My friends and I listen the radio every Saturday morning. _____

2. When I speak, I want you to listen to me! _____

3. What TV show do you listen most often? _____

4. I can't find the remote control. Could you help me look it? _____

5. Please concentrate and listen at the radio program. It is very interesting. _____

6. Why are you looking the floor? What is so interesting? _____

7. Did you lose your wallet? We need to look for it. _____

8. While we are looking for the wallet, we should listen good music. _____

9. Tomorrow we are going to the art museum to look at some art. _____

10. I like to look paintings by Frida Kahlo. _____

CLASS EXERCISE (REVIEW)

Circle the letter of the best answer.

1. Last week I wanted … *American Pie III* but the film was sold out.
   a) to saw   b) see   c) to see   d) saw

2. We need more time … this homework.
   a) to finish   b) finish   c) for finish   d) for to finish

3. On her birthday Lauren likes … receive money … buy new clothes.
   a) to / for   b) to / to   c) (nothing) / for   d) to / (nothing)

4. Last year she tried … her own clothes.
   a) make   b) to made   c) to makes   d) to make

5. Kate is very generous. She doesn't want … money for the work she is doing.
   a) any   b) no   c) some   d) to

6. I want to … in a nice apartment even if I don't have … money right now.
   a) live / some   b) live / any   c) leave / any   d) leave / some

7. Adela and Jose … like … of their new college courses.
   a) really / any   b) very / some   c) really / some   d) very / any

8. We often listen … music, but the neighbors think that the music is … loud.
   a) (nothing) / too   b) at / to   c) to / too   d) (nothing) / to

9. Philippe lost … car keys. Did he look … them in his coat pocket?
   a) is / for   b) his / for   c) is / at   d) his / to

10. I think that you … too much television. You don't have … friends.
    a) listen / some   b) listen / any   c) watch / some   d) watch / any

12 Spelling and Punctuation

Common Spelling Errors

EXERCISE 1 The following words are commonly misspelled. Write the correctly spelled words in the spaces provided.

EXAMPLE: carreer _____career_____

1. futur _____
2. familly _____
3. restaurent _____
4. scool _____
5. visite _____

6. shure _____
7. cours _____
8. verry _____
9. realy _____
10. finaly _____

■ MISSPELLED VERBS

EXERCISE 2 Circle the letter of the correct answer. Then write the correctly spelled word in the space provided.

EXAMPLE: When she was young, Margaret ... a lot about hockey.

a) knowed   b) knews   c) knew _____knew_____

1. These days, Wayne Gretzky generally ... a lot of free time.

a) has   b) haves   c) have _____

2. Wayne Gretzky ... a lot of success when he played for Edmonton's hockey team.

a) haved   b) has   c) had _____

3. The Edmonton Oilers ... home many Stanley Cups.

a) took   b) taked   c) toke _____

4. In 1997, Wayne Gretzky ... to my school.

    a) comed   **b)** came   **c)** cames   _____

5. Gretzky ... our class about hockey fundamentals.

    a) teached   **b)** tought   **c)** taught   _____

6. Last winter, a hockey player from Boston's team ... a big mistake.

    a) made   **b)** mades   **c)** maked   _____

7. After he ... the hockey puck, he accidentally hit another player in the head.

    a) past   **b)** pass   **c)** passed   _____

8. The past form of "think" is ... .

    a) thought   **b)** tought   **c)** thougth   _____

9. Right now I am ... a letter to my sister.

    a) writting   **b)** writhing   **c)** writing   _____

10. We ... for our test, and then we watched the hockey game.

    a) studied   **b)** studyed   **c)** studiied   _____

Punctuation

■ APOSTROPHES (')

Use apostrophes:

- to join a subject and verb together.
- to join an auxiliary with not.
- to indicate possession.

*We're late. **There's** nothing to eat.*
*I **can't** come. They **aren't** very friendly...*
*That is **Simon's** car. **Ross's** computer is new.*

Never use an apostrophe before the *s* at the end of a verb.   Incorrect: *She make's*
                                               Correct: *She makes*

EXERCISE ③ Circle any word that requires an apostrophe, and add the apostrophe.

    EXAMPLE: My (sister's) husband works in Vancouver.

1. Vancouvers in an earthquake zone but most people there dont worry about that.

2. One time my sisters dog, Jed, predicted an earthquake. Jeds tail started to shake and he ran in circles. Usually hes a very quiet animal and he usually doesnt bark.

3. When were older, my sister and I plan to travel to South America together. Shell take time off work and Im going to ask for a long vacation.

4. Shes a dancer and she works with Vancouvers newest dance company. Theyre quite famous.

■ COMMAS (,) AND PERIODS (.)

Use a comma (,)
- to separate words in a series (more than two things). The comma before the final *and* is optional.

  She is kind, considerate, and gentle.
- around interrupting phrases that give additional information about the subject.

  Kevin, a student at Victoria College, says that he never drinks beer.

Use a period (.)
- at the end of a complete sentence.
- after the following titles: *Ms. Mrs. Mr. Dr. Prof.* Do not put a period after *Miss.*

PUNCTUATION TIP

Do not join two complete sentences with a comma.

Incorrect: *Rob is a doctor, he has many patients.*

Correct: *Rob is a doctor. He has many patients.* OR
Rob is a doctor and he has many patients.

EXERCISE ❹ Identify and correct the punctuation errors.

1. The people in my class, sometimes go to movies together.

2. Karen, a girl in my class is very nice.

3. Mr Richman and Mrs Blain work together.

4. The new building need's paint.

5. The new doctor, is a very nice person.

6. Sharon work's with me.

7. We work in the same office, she's a lawyer and I'm an accountant.

8. Sometime's we work with the same clients.

Capitalization

Always capitalize:

1. The first word of a sentence, and the pronoun *I*.
   Joe and I will visit Diane.

2. The word *street, avenue, road, boulevard,* etc., when naming a specific road.
   St. Laurence Boulevard   Yonge Street   Elm Road

3. The days of the week, the months, civic holidays, and historical events.
   Friday   December 25   Christmas Day

4. The names of specific rivers, mountains, lakes, cities, provinces, states.
   Lake Ontario   Castle Mountain   Mississippi River

5. Languages and nationalities.
   Mexican   Spanish   Canadian

6. Titles of specific individuals, and the abbreviations of those titles.
   Dr. King   Officer Williams   President Johnson

7. The names of all religions, nationalities, and tribes.
   Puerto Rican   Buddhist   Iroquois

EXERCISE 5   Add capitals to the following sentences.

EXAMPLE: When I wanted to learn French, I moved to Quebec.

1. Teresa is from puerto rico and she speaks spanish.

2. She's doing a student exchange with a canadian girl.

3. This summer Theresa is living in a house on cedar avenue.

4. She is learning english at redwood school.

5. Generally she goes to school on monday to thursday, but she gets fridays off.

6. Theresa is interested in buddhism and she has several books on the subject.

7. Teresa and i hope to stay in a cabin near black lake during the months of june

   and july.

8. We think that mr. and mrs. Lanoir will rent their cabin to us.

Take Another Look

Ask yourself the following questions. If you don't know an answer, go back and check the appropriate section.

1. Circle the correctly spelled words.

though   future   scool   family   haved   writing

2. Add the necessary punctuation and capitalization to the following sentences.

    a) martin and i hope to learn spanish were going to mexico in february.

    b) hes good at learning languages.

    c) were going to leave on valentines day.

CLASS EXERCISE (REVIEW)

PART A: If the word is misspelled, correct it. If it is correctly spelled, write *C* in the space provided.

1. familly _____

2. writting _____

3. scool _____

4. finally _____

5. haves _____

6. taked _____

7. realy _____

8. very _____

9. cours _____

10. maked _____

PART B: Add the necessary punctuation and capital letters to the following sentences. The number of punctuation changes is indicated in brackets.

EXAMPLE: [2] Last April, adelas mother became very ill because of exposure to pesticides.

11. [5] Adela has dual citizenship shes mexican and canadian.

12. [2] She moved to canada in july.

13. [3] Did you know that ms santos is an environmental activist?

14. [4] She wrote a letter to president bush to protest against americas global warming policies.

15. [5] Next friday shell appear at a rally on yonge street in toronto.

Review of Units 7 to 12

A, An, The

CLASS EXERCISE A

Put *a, an, the,* or *X* in the space provided.

1. I have _____ good friends. Carlos is _____ very nice man. On my birthday, he gave me _____ expensive necklace.

2. Kim needs _____ doctor. _____ doctor in that clinic is very nice. I hope to be _____ nurse one day.

3. I have _____ idea. Let's visit _____ Calgary. We can go to _____ Calgary Zoo.

4. Katya is expecting _____ baby. If _____ baby is a girl, she will be very happy. Katya likes _____ name Margo.

5. _____ French is not _____ easy language to learn. Many people speak three languages in _____ Switzerland.

Plurals and Articles

CLASS EXERCISE B

Circle and correct the errors in plurals or article usage in the following sentences. Each sentence has one error.

EXAMPLE: I have (an) nice teacher. _____ *a* _____

1. There are fifty person in my class. _____

2. This is my first years in university. _____

3. I want to be teacher. _____

4. I take Spanish and others subjects. _____

5. I want to teach small childrens.   _____

6. Do you think that a children need love?   _____

7. All of my course are interesting.   _____

8. I don't have an other plan for my future.   _____

9. Every evening I study alot.   _____

10. I have some very goods friends.   _____

Modals

CLASS EXERCISE C

Circle the letter of the best answer.

1. What ... for lunch today?
   a) you would like   **b)** should you like   **c)** would you like

2. Martin ... because his client is waiting.
   a) must leaves   **b)** has to leave   **c)** have to leave

3. Your sister ... the lobster. It is delicious.
   a) should to try   **b)** should tries   **c)** should try

4. ... the seafood?
   a) Can she eats   **b)** Can she can eat   **c)** Can she eat

5. Why ... until midnight?
   a) should he work   **b)** he should work   **c)** should he works

6. ... overtime again?
   a) He has to work   **b)** Does he have to work   **c)** Has he to work

7. Martin ... to a restaurant with us tomorrow.
   a) can come   **b)** can comes   **c)** can to come

8. He ... for a court case tonight.
   a) must to prepare   **b)** have to prepare   **c)** must prepare

9. I ... study tonight.
   a) don't have to   **b)** not have to   **c)** haven't to

10. When he was a child, Martin ... German, but now he can't.
   a) could speak   **b)** can speak   **c)** can spoke

Comparatives and Superlatives

CLASS EXERCISE D

Complete these sentences with the correct comparative or superlative form of the adjectives. Do not use *as … as*.

EXAMPLE: (tall) A giraffe is _____*taller than*_____ a horse.

1. (expensive) I think violins are _____ guitars.

2. (careful) Annie is _____ her brother.

3. (bad) Many people think the Spice Girls was one of _____ _____ bands in the world.

4. (nice) Judy is _____ her sister Gloria.

5. (loud) That is _____ band in Los Angeles!

6. (good) Billie Holliday was _____ singer in the world.

7. (easy) My job is _____ your job.

8. (tasty) Indian food is _____ British food.

9. (violent) Sometimes music videos are _____ regular movies.

10. (good) My father thinks that John Lennon's music is _____ _____ Paul McCartney's music.

Verb Tenses: Question and Negative Forms

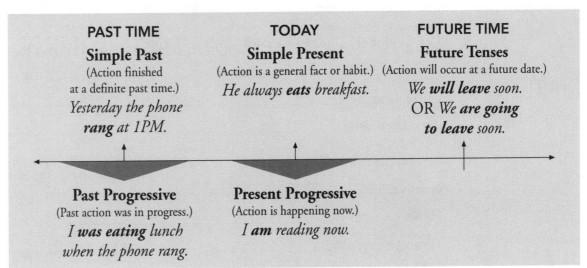

PAST TIME	TODAY	FUTURE TIME
Simple Past (Action finished at a definite past time.) *Yesterday the phone **rang** at 1PM.*	**Simple Present** (Action is a general fact or habit.) *He always **eats** breakfast.*	**Future Tenses** (Action will occur at a future date.) *We **will leave** soon.* OR *We **are going to leave** soon.*
Past Progressive (Past action was in progress.) *I **was eating** lunch when the phone rang.*	**Present Progressive** (Action is happening now.) *I **am** reading now.*	

CLASS EXERCISE E

Write a negative statement. Then write a yes/no question and an information question. (The exact answer is in bold).

EXAMPLE: The store closes **at 5 PM**.   (simple present)

Negative: *The store does not close at 5 PM.*

Yes/ No question: *Does the store close at 5 PM?*

Information question: *When does the store close?*

1. Maruka lives **in Spain**.   (simple present)

Negative: _____

Yes/No Question: _____

Information question: _____

2. Mr. Lee went to India **last summer**.   (simple past)

Negative: _____

Yes/No Question: _____

Information question: _____

3. Kevin is visiting **Maruka** right now.   (present progressive)

Negative: _____

Yes/No Question: _____

Information question: _____

4. We were walking **on the beach** when the lightning started.   (past progressive)

Negative: _____

Yes/No Question: _____

Information question: _____

5. They will meet us **next week** for lunch.   (future)

Negative: _____

Yes/No Question: _____

Information question: _____

6. Maruka can speak **five** languages.   (modal: can)

Negative: _____

Yes/No Question: _____

Information question: _____

1 Websites with Grammar Exercises

If you want additional practice, you can find many grammar exercises on the following websites.

Look carefully on each site for "grammar exercises" or "grammar tests" or look for the grammar point that you want to practice.

www.esl-classroom.com

esl.about.com/library/quiz/blgrammarquiz.htm

www.eslcafe.com (click on "quizzes.")

www.englishday.com (click on "tests")

www.english-at-home.com (click on "grammar")

teslj.org/links/

On the following website, enter the site and go to the "companion website" page. Then you will find exercises and tests.

www.longman.com/grammarexpress

If these sites are no longer in service, then just go to your search engine and write "ESL grammar practice" in the search space.

2 Frequently Asked Questions

■ WHEN DO I ADD "S" TO VERBS?

Add "s" to present tense verbs that follow a third-person singular subject. Third-person singular refers to **one** person, place or thing, except *you* and *I*.

Every morning Sharon walks to work.	(One person)
The problem deserves careful consideration.	(One idea)
The poolroom has many tables.	(One place)

Do not add "s" to

• verbs that follow *you*, *we*, *I*, or *they*.	*They walk to work.*
• past tense verbs	*Sharon walked to work.*
• future tense verbs	*Sharon will walk to work.*
• modals	*Sharon can walk to work.*

■ WHAT IS THE DIFFERENCE BETWEEN *DO*, *DOES*, AND *DID*?

These are forms of the verb "to do."   *He <u>does</u> his homework. I <u>do</u> the dishes.*

Do, *does*, and *did* are also auxiliaries that are added to question and negative verb forms.

For question or negative forms:

■ Simple Present

• Add *do* to simple present tense questions and negative forms.

You work a lot.	**Do** *you work a lot?*	*You **do**n't work a lot.*

• Add *does* to simple present tense question and negative forms *when the subject is third-person singular.*

She works a lot.	**Does** *she work a lot?*	*She **does**n't work a lot.*

■ Simple Past

• Add *did* to simple past tense question and negative forms.

Yesterday we ate corn.	**Did** *you eat corn?*	*You **did**n't eat corn.*

CAN I PUT *HAVE* OR *HAS* BEFORE PAST TENSE VERBS?

No.

When you write in the past tense, simply change the verb from the present form to the past form.

Present tense	**Past tense**
We go out.	*We **went** out.*
The doctor works hard.	*The doctor **worked** hard.*
She has many problems.	*She **had** many problems.*

But there is a verb tense that you may learn more about in a future course. It is called the "present perfect" tense and it is formed with *have* or *has* + the past participle.

(The past participle is in the third column of irregular verb lists. For example, the past participle of *go* is *gone*. The past participle of regular verbs is simply the *ed* form.)

Examples of the present perfect tense:
   *Many astronauts **have explored** outer space. John Glenn **has been** to space twice.*

The present perfect tense is used in two different ways.

1. Past action(s) occurred at an indefinite past time.
   *He **has been** to Mexico three times.*   (We don't know exactly when he went to Mexico.)

   Key words: once, twice, many times, already…

2. An action started in the past and continues to the present time.
   *He **has lived** in Canada since 1994.*   (He came in 1994 and he is still in Canada.)

   Key words: since, for, ever, yet, my whole life, …

Do not confuse the present perfect tense with the simple past tense. When you tell a story about a past event, use the simple past!

When I was young, I have ~~learned~~ to play the violin. (learned)

CAN I PUT *FOR + TO* TOGETHER?

No.

Never put *for* and *to* together!

She is ready ~~for to have~~ her massage. (to have)

Generally, when a verb is followed by another verb, use the infinitive (to + base form) of the second verb.

*We really need **to talk**.*
                 infinitive

■ DO SOME QUESTIONS HAVE NO AUXILIARY?

Yes.

When *who* and *what* ask about the <u>subject</u> of a question, no auxiliary is needed.

Simon lives with Angela.   **The car** needs a new engine.

Who *lives with Simon?*   **What** *needs a new engine?*

When *who(m)** and *what* ask about the <u>object</u> of a question, you must put an auxiliary.

Simon lives with **Angela**.   The car needs **a new engine**.

Who(m)* **_does_** *Simon live with?*   **What** **_does_** *the car need?*

*Note: whom is rarely used in spoken English.

You could practice by trying the following exercise.

PRACTICE EXERCISE

Write an information question. The answer to the question is in bold.

<u>EXAMPLES:</u>   Terry lives with **his mother**.   Who   *does Terry live with?*

             Terry lives with his mother.   Who   *lives with his mother?*

1. **Jean** is very nice.   Who _____

2. She visited **her mother**.   Who _____

3. **The window** needs a new frame.   What _____

4. The window needs **a new frame**.   What _____

5. **Mr. Guzzo** owns a factory.   Who _____

6. Mr. Guzzo owns **a factory**.   What _____

3 Non-Count Nouns

You cannot put a number before a non-count noun. These types of nouns have no plural form. Here are some of the most common non-count nouns:

CATEGORIES These nouns designate a category of objects.		FOOD		ABSTRACT NOUNS	
change (money)	luggage	bread	milk	advice	research
clothing	mail	cheese	salt	effort	time (free time,
equipment	money	coffee / tea	sugar	evidence	extra time)
furniture	music	ice	water	information	
homework	work	meat	wine	knowledge	

EXAMPLE: *We need some <u>informations</u>.*
Information is a non-count noun. It cannot end in -s.

To indicate a number of items, you must specify that you need "a piece of …", "a slice of …," etc.

*I need **some bread**.*   *I want **two slices** of bread.*
*We need **some information**.*   *We need **one piece** of information.*

PRACTICE EXERCISE

Put *a* or *an* before count nouns. (Remember to put *an* before count nouns that begin with a vowel.) Put *some* before non-count nouns and plural nouns.

EXAMPLE: I live in _____*an*_____ old building. I put _____*some*_____ furniture in the basement.

1. Eric has _____ homework. He has to finish _____ assignment about the Roman Empire. He needs to find _____ information at the library. There is _____ interesting book about Rome in the fiction section. The book tells _____ story about Julius Caesar. It gives _____ evidence that Caesar poisoned the king of Egypt.

2. Steve would like _____ cup of coffee with _____ milk and _____ sugar. He wants to find _____ job, and he needs _____ advice about his career. He would like to start his own business, but he needs _____ money to do that.

4 Irregular Verb List

The most frequently used past tense verbs are in bold. For this course, you will rarely use past participles.

BASE FORM	SIMPLE PAST	Past Participle	BASE FORM	SIMPLE PAST	Past Participle
arise	**arose**	arisen	eat	**ate**	eaten
awake	**awoke**	awoken	fall	**fell**	fallen
be	**was, were**	been	feed	fed	fed
bear	bore	born	feel	**felt**	felt
become	**became**	become	fight	**fought**	fought
begin	**began**	begun	find	**found**	found
bend	bent	bent	fly	**flew**	flown
bet	bet	bet	forget	**forgot**	forgotten
bite	**bit**	bitten	forgive	forgave	forgiven
bleed	bled	bled	freeze	froze	frozen
blow	**blew**	blown	get	**got**	got, gotten
break	**broke**	broken	give	**gave**	given
bring	**brought**	brought	go	**went**	gone
build	**built**	built	grow	**grew**	grown
buy	**bought**	bought	hang	hung	hung
catch	**caught**	caught	have	**had**	had
choose	**chose**	chosen	hear	**heard**	heard
come	**came**	come	hide	hid	hidden
cost	**cost**	cost	hit	**hit**	hit
cut	**cut**	cut	hold	**held**	held
dig	dug	dug	hurt	**hurt**	hurt
do	**did**	done	keep	**kept**	kept
draw	drew	drawn	know	**knew**	known
dream	**dreamed / dreamt**[1]	dreamed / dreamt	lay	laid	laid
drink	**drank**	drunk	lead	led	led
drive	**drove**	driven	learn	**learned / learnt**	learned / learnt

1. Many verbs have two past forms. Both past forms are correct.

© Longman

BASE FORM	SIMPLE PAST	Past Participle	BASE FORM	SIMPLE PAST	Past Participle
leave	**left**	left	sit	**sat**	sat
lend	lent	lent	sleep	**slept**	slept
let	let	let	slide	slid	slid
lie (down)[2]	lay	lain	speak	**spoke**	spoken
light	lit	lit	speed	sped	sped
lose	**lost**	lost	spend	**spent**	spent
make	**made**	made	spin	spun	spun
mean	**meant**	meant	spread	spread	spread
meet	**met**	met	spring	sprang	sprung
mistake	mistook	mistaken	stand	**stood**	stood
pay	**paid**	paid	steal	**stole**	stolen
prove	proved	proven	stick	stuck	stuck
put	**put**	put	sting	stung	stung
quit	**quit**	quit	strike	struck	struck
read[3]	**read**	read	swear	swore	sworn
ride	**rode**	ridden	sweep	swept	swept
ring	**rang**	rung	swim	**swam**	swum
rise	rose	risen	swing	swung	swung
run	**ran**	run	take	**took**	taken
say	**said**	said	teach	**taught**	taught
see	**saw**	seen	tear	tore	torn
sell	**sold**	sold	tell	**told**	told
send	**sent**	sent	think	**thought**	thought
set	set	set	throw	**threw**	thrown
shake	shook	shaken	understand	**understood**	understood
shine	shone	shone	upset	upset	upset
shoot	shot	shot	wake	**woke**	woken
show	showed	shown	wear	**wore**	worn
shut	shut	shut	win	**won**	won
sing	**sang**	sung	withdraw	withdrew	withdrawn
sink	sank	sunk	write	**wrote**	written

2. When *lie* means "to make a false statement," then it is a regular verb: *lie, lied, lied.*
3. The present (base) form of *read* is pronounced: "reed." The past form is pronounced "red."

114.

83

Index